Prosilio

— *Toward the Sun* —

CAROL OLSEN LAMONDA

Order this book online at www.trafford.com
or email orders@trafford.com

Most Trafford titles are also available at major online book retailers.

Printed in the United States of America.

ISBN: 978-1-4269-4918-0 (sc)
ISBN: 978-1-4269-4919-7 (hc)
ISBN: 978-1-4269-4920-3 (e)

Library of Congress Control Number: 2010941115

Trafford rev. 01/19/2011

 www.trafford.com

North America & International
toll-free: 1 888 232 4444 (USA & Canada)
phone: 250 383 6864 ♦ fax: 812 355 4082

Prosilio

In Greek, Prosilio means, "Toward the Sun"

June 13, 2010

A little girl was born on June 10, 2010. My son and daughter-in-law named her Philanthe Bella. She weighed a lucky seven pounds, eleven ounces, and will be going home to a nursery chock full of too many outfits, stuffed animals and the very best furniture. She has been loved and anticipated for nine long months by parents who have yet to let her out of their comforting arms.

She will carry the name of my great aunt Philanthe who lived such a hard life, yet persevered and endured so her future generations could prosper. Her Greek heritage has been diluted and altered by three generations of Americans who added the strength and traditions of Native Americans, Norwegians, Italians, Poles, Scots, and English. She will play with her cousins who are Danish and Argentine as well as Norwegian and Greek. She will be an American woman who will someday know the story of the determined Greek woman who lived a century before her who refused to be darkened by the shadows of her life. Philanthe Bella will learn to leave the shadows behind her and always strive for the warmth and light of the sun.

Dedication

To my husband Bruce who harped on me for forty some years saying, "You know, you should write a book."

And to my mother who protected me from all that lurked in the shadows by making me face the sun.

Author's Note to Readers:

The summers at the farm in New Paltz are my recollections of the time spent with my family, my cousins and their families. The flashbacks to the murders that occurred the year of my birth are based on multiple accounts from the *Kingston Freeman* and the *New York Times* and stories told by family members. The events leading up to the tragedy are imagined to find motives for the series of murders. This family memoir is not meant to be a record of the crimes; rather it is my attempt to make sense of them. The juxtaposition of carefree summers and horrific murders is a deliberate attempt to present life in its balance of good and evil.

Preface

During the ravages of World War II, while soldiers were killing in the noble names of peace, justice and love of country, four senseless murders wounded the Takis family. On a Friday and Saturday in September of 1944, a jealous husband performed a Greek tragedy by killing his wife and her uncle with the blades of a single pair of scissors separated to become weapons. His children were left lifeless, gassed, on a bed in their Queens apartment.

My mom and aunts spared us the family tragedy that occurred the very year when my cousins, Jimmy and Kenny, and I were born. Turning from the grief of deaths, the young mothers focused on the new lives that began that year. These matriarchs were brave enough to offer us a carefree summer at a farmhouse in New Paltz, which had been the scene of a jealous murder of Uncle Petros.

Now, half a century later, we orphaned cousins, baby boomers all, tried to piece the story together through news articles and family anecdotes. The ten cousins reconnected at our mothers' funerals in 2006, 2007 and 2008, and between consoling words, we smiled and relived our summer of 1956. The reveries of a happy and carefree vacation always led to the admission of our youthful ignorance of the murders. The generation who could have told us was gone. A solemn dirge with a tragic melody played as background music as we solemnly acknowledged the responsibility to investigate and answer the question, "How do you go on when a tragedy of four murders tears the fabric of family?" Now, we, the cousins, graduated to the last generation, assumed the task of investigating the murders of four people we did not know-- four people who should have danced at our weddings and brought gifts to our children's baptisms.

In researching and sharing, we have rediscovered our family roots and have come to admire Philanthe, my great aunt, who was eyewitness to the death of Petros, her younger brother. She survived only to learn that the murderer, her son-in-law, had killed her daughter and two granddaughters the night before.

The answer is in the life of Philanthe, who was born in an isolated village in Greece called Prosilio, which translates "Toward the Sun." This woman, long gone, taught us the lesson of survival. You keep looking toward the sun, letting the shadows fall behind you. The light of day came in spite of the dark tragedy. The family knew to bury their grief along with the dead. Words did not exist to speak what was so unthinkable and therefore untellable. The living simply faced the rising sun and went on. If the murders were mentioned, they were quickly hushed, yet the victims surrounded the family like restless ghosts who would not lie comfortably in their graves.

The family lived knowing but not acknowledging the *dolofonia*, the killing, and took the details of the quadruple murder with them when they died. They were too close to the event to tell the tale. The love of life drowned out the collective cries of the senseless deaths. The Old Greeks were Philanthe and her brothers and sisters. They lived the horror. My mom and aunts were supporting actresses to a tragic play knowing the main characters of killer and victims. They all distanced themselves from the sad events as they created and expanded their own families despite the obliteration of four family relatives. We cousins were mildly disinterested in the supposed murder of some relatives. Grief and details fades with each generation. Our children and grandchildren will only emote surprise and awe that there could have been such a murder in the family sometime in the distant past.

The Matriarchs were my mom, Aunt Helen, Aunt Chris and Aunt Carrie. All four are now gone. Mom, Helen and Chris died within twenty-one months of each other. Aunt Carrie had Alzheimer's disease; her mind died first, but her body outlasted her dear friends by more than a year. These strong ladies were the middle generation. They were the children of Europeans, descendents of Greek and Norwegian culture. They were the luncheon meat in the sandwich of the generations. Born to immigrants, they were the bridge to the Old Greeks and the Old Square-Heads and our only contact to Greece and Norway. They were Americans with the flavor of the old country.

We, the cousins, were American, through and through. Born in Brooklyn, we were so busy being American, listening to *American Bandstand* and living the *Happy Days* teenage years that we forgot to ask questions about the murders. We expected our parents to always be there, a living vault of heritage and history. Now they are gone, and questions remain unanswered.

Fifty-five years had to pass for two generations of shock waves to subside. The Old Greeks died. Our aunts, children of the Old Greeks, became the matriarchs and died when we cousins were too involved in raising our own children to believe in our parents' mortality. My cousins, the older generation in their fifties and sixties, inherited unearned titles of matriarchs and patriarchs. In reminiscing about our days at the farm in New Paltz, we ironically pursued a quest to uncover the facts about the murders. We must now speak the unspeakable so the ghosts can go away. It is time to leave the shadows behind us and walk toward the sun.

The Village of Prosilio

"YiYia, you make the best toast." I complimented my grandmother on the Herculean effort to offer the best her palsied hands could create. The browned bread was her gift from the heart; it was sustenance born of love and much struggle. It was good too. Thinking back, there was food for both body and mind in this simple meal.

My grandmother, like her sister-in-law Philanthe, knew the recipe that was more wisdom than ingredients. There is an art to making toast. It can't be too light or too dark. It has to be snatched from the toaster at the very moment when the bread is Army Khaki, but not brown. It has to smell sweet and enticing as it does the moment just before someone yells, "The toast is burning."

If you are making toast with an unfamiliar toaster, you might have to burn the toast in order to readjust the settings on the toaster or the temperature of the fire. Making toast is the embodiment of the Greek philosophy of doing everything in moderation. Not too hot, not too cold. In order to get things "just right" in life, you need to learn from a host of mistakes and experiences.

Greeks try to live on that invisible swirling midline of the yin yang sign. Contrary to the Duchess of Windsor's famous quote that a woman can never be too thin or too rich, the Greeks believed a woman should be not too skinny or not too fat. A man shouldn't be too poor or too rich. Life is to be lived in the middle of a very uncertain road on a journey to some unknown destination. Everything is to be done in moderation, and we all walk precariously on that "tight rope" of "just right." If we veer too far to the right or to the left, we find ourselves in the abyss of too little or too much. If we do, the whole universe has to readjust to put itself back in the comfort zone.

Philanthe's life was too much on the dark side. That is why she, the phototropic "lover of flowers," always leaned toward the sun.

When my mother signed my sixth grade blue zippered autograph book that each graduate got from Columbus Avenue Elementary School, she did not write on the first page nor did she turn to the last page. She did not pick a bright page or a dull one. She opened the pristine album to the middle and wrote on a pale yellow page: "Always walk toward the sun, so the shadows will fall behind you." The remainder of the book was filled with cute, popular messages of luck and silliness. It would take me more than half a century to realize the secret of life my mom shared with an almost teenager. Always turn toward the sun. Flowers instinctively do. Animals respond in the same way. My cat seeks out that morning sunbeam and claims the plot of land as his own. The chocolate lab, Diva, rises when the sun does, wagging her tail to go outside to greet the day. That's where the story of Philanthe begins.

Prosilio, in Greek, translates "Towards the Sun," and Prosilio is the name of the village where the Fates chose to begin the story of my great aunt Philanthe, an epic filled with challenges that were rewarded in future generations of children and grandchildren who were fortunate enough to bask in the light.

I am reminded of two myths that deal with this path of moderation and the sun. In one Phaeton, who is the son of Apollo and a mortal woman, asks his god/father for a special favor. He asks the god of light and reason to drive the sun chariot that strong stallions pull across the morning sky. Apollo wisely warns him that he is not ready to do that. When Phaeton insists, Apollo reneges and tells his son to stay on the middle path. "If you go too high, you will set fire to the heavens. If you go too close to the earth, you will scorch the earth." Unable to hold the challenging steeds, Phaeton loses control and dies in a fiery blaze.

In another myth, a man-bull creature called the Minotaur imprisoned Daedalus and his son, Icarus, in The Labyrinth. To escape from this prison on the island of Crete, Daedalus, who was an inventor, fashioned wings made of feathers and wax. He warns his son Icarus that he must follow his father and not stray from the middle path. If he flew too high or too low, the wings would not work. Icarus strayed too high, and the sun melted the wax. He flew too low, and the spray of the ocean weighted down the feathers. Icarus crashed into the sea leaving his father to mourn the son who did not heed his advice.

We must walk toward the sun on a course of moderation. Extremes, in Greek mythology, can end in dire consequences. Philanthe's journey from Prosilio took her away from the sun, through the dark and back into the light.

My grandfather, his little sister Philanthe, and their eight siblings were born in this small village, which wasn't always called Prosilio. They grew up in the village when it was known by its Turkish name: Strudza. In the little mountain village high above the seaside town of Gytheon, there were few trees or flowers. Only the hardy olive trees clung to the sloping land. In any direction, one could see stark mountains, a range higher than the uphill slanted perch on which the Tritakis farm stood so precariously. The distant mountains were so stately and so far reaching that their colors blended into a dusty gray and then an even dustier gray. Eventually, it became impossible to tell where the mountaintops ended and the sky began.

It was here that Philanthe was born to Nicholas and Kalliope. In this land that was home to language, the names of these people are important. Nicholas meant "victorious" and Kalliope meant, "muse of epic stories." When one is a farmer on an arid mountain, you need to be victorious over the land. Perhaps what keeps a man working day after day is the knowledge that his story will go on and on as long as the family goes on. The wind hums through the few acres of olive trees, and the smell of the salt air is proof that the town and the Aegean Sea is but a few miles down that steep and windy road that spirals up this imposing mountain. The work of tired hands is repaid in the promise of the next generation of children, their children and their children's children. Ten children were born in this simple, cool bermed farmhouse and were nourished by the food and animals just out the back door.

Only three of those children stayed in Greece. Five of the six male children made their way down that steep mountain and beyond the Town of Gytheon and across the Atlantic to Brooklyn.

Philanthe means "lover of flowers," but she was born in a place where flowers were a luxury. The rich people in Gytheon by the sea below had gardens with flowers. Here the flowering vegetables and fruits of cucumbers, melons, and tomatoes were the only colors that broke the landscape of dirt, rocks, and short trees of olives and figs that were sturdy enough to withstand the winds and exist on little moisture. Perhaps it is her name that was her destiny to leave this tiny village for the town below and the world beyond the sea. Perhaps she longed for flowers.

The village is small, and villagers travel from farm to farm and to their village center on foot, on donkeys or on carts pulled by donkeys. They still do a century later although small, fuel-efficient cars now ascend the mountain. Relatives and tourists climb the mountain because Prosilio is a destination, not for those on a journey. There is no where to go except higher and further into the Peloponnesian Mountains, and there nothing except, perhaps, the ancient gods and the fates who watch us play out our destiny below.

When my mother was there in 1980, the entire village of eighty came to the central plaza to meet the American daughter of Aristomenes, my grandfather, who lived on the Tritakis farm as his nephew's wife still does today. There were only eight children, schooled by the Priest's wife, in this village about to be deserted by youth. It will be the ghost town of the last century until the tourists move up the mountain from the quaint touristy fishing village with the large Laryssion Hotel overlooking the harbor. Someday soon condos and Smart Cars will replace the small homesteads and donkeys of today.

At the village center, most will stop to pray at the small sanctuary that is about the size of a one-car garage. There are four benches facing the altar with icons hanging on the walls. The saints stare down at you from their tilted heads wearing golden haloes like heavenly Easter bonnets. They appear to be dressed up for a celebration for which only a few select guests received invitations. Tall, thin, red candles light the enclosure in an amber glow, and there is a box to make donations. It is a chapel where the pilgrim comes to pray, not to hear a sermon. A feeling that the visitor is in the presence of royalty can be sensed in this humblest of stone chapels. Men and women visit, deposit their prayers and leave the space to the unseen holy. It is a place of solitary communion with God, unless there is a festival; then the ceremony spills outside of the small enclosure.

When outside, the sun and the heat remind one that humans must try to carry that cool peace and comfort out into a world that sometimes harms us with its unholy deeds of mortal men.

The Priest is not here. He is home on his farm with his family, but everyone knows where he lives. If there is occasion like a baptism, wedding or funeral, he will be summoned, if he doesn't know already. If someone is sick or hurt, he has already said prayers and will visit that family. He tends to the joy and sins of all.

Although unattended, the chapel is the hub of the village flanked by a small *taverna* that is a gathering place. It is about the same size as the sanctuary, but its fourth wall never constricts its enclosure; one wall opens to a counter connecting the inside and the outside. On a dirt or stone patio are four simple weatherworn chairs around three, square tables. Greeks prefer to eat al fresco, under the sky or arbor.

Here villagers, at least once a day, will assemble to share a glass of *Ouzo* or *Retsina*, a wine made of pine pitch, or a soda of freshly squeezed *limoni* while they play Backgammon or Chess. Some men sit sideways on their chairs with their feet outstretched as they fidget with their worry beads. The news of the day is passed from person to person without the need of a printed page. Gossip ripens as the vine of conversation grows. The men discuss politics and events; later they relate their authoritative version to the family at the next meal. The women will add details gleaned from the marketplace.

There is no school, no hospital, no police or fire department. There is no need. Nothing here can burn except the three wooden tables and chairs at the *taverna*, and when everyone knows everyone, there is no need for police. One does not commit crimes against a neighbor who struggles as you do. If you break the rules of society, then the village banishes you or punishes you with ridicule or isolation. Sometimes it protects you, as it did Philanthe's family.

Here children of large families have friends at home and friends down the road. The strong teenagers will even hike down the fifteen kilometers to the town below where they can go to the *agora* (market), shops, watch the ferry that crosses to Hania, the port in Crete, and fish and swim from the shore that defines the length of the town of Gytheon. Imagine the long, steep walk home, with or without a donkey, as the sun sets behind them on the shimmering Aegean Sea. They drag themselves up to their parents' home, slowly and reluctantly. They have already seen what life is like at the foot of the mountain. Someday they will go there, perhaps beyond. Someday they might even travel to Sparta and Athens. Someday they might go to American where everyone eats in restaurants and buys clothes in stores. The village remained suspended in time until the turn of the century brought its technology of Internet and satellites to invade its isolated and insulated space. Youth will be fast-forwarded into the chaos of the modern world.

A century before, Philanthe, the youngest girl of the Tritakis family, left the quiet, simple life of her family's mountain village. She should have known better than to try to outwit The Fates. Violence would rip her from the quiet countryside of Prosilio and follow her to America. Her destiny will be to mentor a generation of strong matriarchs. Her suffering will be the sermon for success. Like her birthplace's name, *Prosilio*, Philanthe will always face toward the sun. The shadows will be left behind her.

Philanthe Tritakis Kontolefa

The Ancient Greeks

The ancient Greeks believed that the Three Fates sat on the edge of the "Other World," weaving our lives into a complex tapestry forming a design that they, not mortals, could see. The fates were the three Greek Goddesses of Destiny known as the Moirae. These timeless old hags wove the threads of destiny that control our lives. The Fates were: Clotho, who spun the Thread of Life; Lachesis, who allotted the length of the yarn, and Atropos, who snipped the string ending one's mortal life. People dangled on threads of varied colors, strength and length that would weave in and out of the threads of others. Each life entered the design of the human epic. Figuratively, we were hanging on by strings that tangled and then separated from time to time. We may connect for a time and then move on to weave into some other life, forming patterns that only the fates could see. Sometimes the threads became so twisted and matted that only a sharp implement could separate the tangled knot leaving a blood red blotch on the landscape of lives cut shorter than they should be.

As I write the story of Philanthe, I write the story of my family, my culture, and all of humanity who are woven into the picture. What is this tapestry? Only the weaver knows. Imagine all of us in a thread of some color, hue and intensity. Some threads are fine, expensive, delicate, thick or thin. I would say that Philanthe's thread was of heavy-duty cotton that could withstand adversity. The color of her string would be dark, but not black. Perhaps it would be the color of Kalamata Olives or a very dark Concord grape or the Aegean Sea on a moonless night. It certainly wouldn't be pastel. No, her life was anything but pastel. Her life thread had to be bold, but not ostentatious. Her life thread had to be strong enough to hold her and her family together through adoption, desertion, immigration, and loss of brother, daughter, and grandchildren to a senseless murder. The fates were not kind to Philanthe. In her life she could not imagine the picture of strength she was to her family. Like impressionistic dots, only time and distance will reveal the intricate design she played in the final picture.

Our lives only entwined a few times, but her survival influenced all of us who shared summers at the farmhouse.

The Matriarchs

The word *matriarch* conjures an image of an elderly, matronly woman wearing pearls or brooch that brings attention to ample bust cleavage and multiple chins. Either that or the matriarch is a wrinkled stick figure wearing a velvet or silk outfit that falls like a dress on a hanger. I envision matriarchs captured in over-sized portraits within a frame of carved wood and gilt. The word itself implies wealth, power, and privilege. It is a term reserved for the aristocracy and the oligarchy. Matriarchs appear to be strong women. They may or not be. Perhaps they just out-lived their husbands and earned the respect of age and position through endurance.

The matriarchs in my family may have had pearls and brooches and fine costumes, but they did not wear them comfortably. My mom, Min (short for Minerva), and my aunt Helen, and my "aunts" Carrie and Christine were matriarchs in their thirties. Jeans, khaki and cotton were their uniforms, and plain gold wedding bands were their jewels. They were matriarchs with husbands and children who were not princely or precocious. These four women ruled the summer vacations at the New Paltz farm of my childhood while their husbands worked in the city.

Like the Iroquois, these women ruled our world with enlightened despotism. Later these four women became the strong widows who guided our family until they could not take another step nor offer advice. Tradition and history were archived in their minds. When they were gone, they challenged the next generation to seek answers to the unasked questions. The quest to find out more about Philanthe, the Greek mother of Carrie and aunt of Min and Helen, and the murder at the farm house taught us how strong a woman can be when the role of matriarch is earned by turning away from tragedy and moving on.

Life has a way of fast-forwarding us from teenager to matriarch. I think it was when Aunt Helen lay helpless and frail in the nursing home bed that we cousins realized that we had checker-jumped from the youngest generation to the oldest. We had done so without ceremony or tutelage. All of a sudden, we were the ones to carry on without our mothers. We were orphaned leaders who had inherited a foreign kingdom. In hospital rooms that reeked of Pine Sol and urine, the children of the matriarchs grappled with the unanswered questions as their mothers wrestled with the angels. The angels won.

I was sure mom would live forever. At eighty-five she looked and acted sixty. Helen, mom's sister, was five years older. It was rumored that some grandfather, great or great-great, had lived to be 116. I had ignored the calendar. I had defied the fates. I knew that Mom and Helen would die someday, but not now. Not my mom. Even when they each got cancer, I was sure they would recover. They didn't.

My mom should have been invincible and immortal like the goddess of wisdom, war, and weaving for which she was named. I was sure that Aunt Helen would find herself on a Smuckers' Jar with Willard Scott remarking how lively and spry she was when she reached 100. She only made it to ninety-one. When my mom, her younger sister, died of lung cancer, Helen had lost the remainder of her family, her best friend and her sparring partner.

If Aunt Helen was the smartest, then mom was the brightest. Mom loved being right and most popular, and Helen loved mom. They were opposites sharing only the very strong gene of Greek hospitality. They were the hubs in a wheel of family. They were the ties to the "Old Greeks."

Sisterly love was the unstated message in the sibling bossing that went on. Aunt Helen was smart, really smart. She was an Arista and Mensa member. Mom was smart, but she was not as smart as Helen. "How can she not read books?" mom would ask me. Mom read three books a week. Helen would always lament, "Min's prettier than I am." It was a loving contest of one-up-womanship. My mom would harp on Helen's shortcomings to the rest of her friends, but she loved her sister. If she could make Helen appear foolish, then mom felt smarter.

Surrounding the bed, we told stories of our moms as my sister Kathy, my cousins and I sat vigil as Helen lay there dying of Pancreatic Cancer. The peripheral chatter in that small cubicle of a nursing home was our magic incantation to ward off the presence of death that was visible in the hollow, sunken eyes of the skeleton that lay motionless under a sandwich of covers. Our eyes darted from a dozing patient, to weepy visitors' eyes, to the blue monitor with its jagged lines to the television with picture but no sound. To obliterate the deafening silence and awkward eye contact, we would recall the times shared at the farm. Our funny memories breathed life into the sisters who hovered on both sides of heaven. We challenged the mechanical noises of death, the clicks and hums of medical technology, with anecdotes of life. We dared not stop talking for fear that the silence would signify surrender.

My sister and I, in unison at times, told our favorite Min and Helen and the "fluton" story. One day, Helen called my mom, as she did daily or sometimes hourly. They lived but two miles away from each other, and, although they visited or shared a meal frequently, they always checked in with each other as best friends would to share the news of the day. Three of the four aunts lived within two miles of each other. Aunt Carrie lived in Brooklyn, but visited by phone. Family ties were the telephone lines.

My mom would always call me every night at five. She would pour herself a glass of very dry white wine, which originally came from a box, but was re-poured into a nicer carafe that she kept cool in the refrigerator. She would then dial my number and like a record put to the turntable, she would tell me what she did, what her friends did, and then ask, "What's new with you?" She would add my news to her news and then call Kathy, my sister, Kenny, my brother, Aunt Helen and Aunt Christine, and sometimes Aunt Carrie. The purpose of the medley of wine flavored calls would be to brag in an unspoken contest of "My kid is better than your kid."

Anyway, this day Aunt Helen called to spread the great news about her neighbor getting a "Fluton." "Jean got a fluton from Weidy's Furniture Store," Helen blurted out, as if she were revealing a state secret.

"Helen," mom corrected her older sister. "It's not fluton. It's called a futon."

"Yeah, yeah, so Jean got this fluton, and she's putting…"

Mom, always the one to point out Helen's shortcomings, interrupted, "It's a futon, Helen. There is no 'L' in futon. It's Futon. F-U-"

This time Helen, tired of the spelling lesson and wanting to blurt out the news about who was coming to visit and sleep on the bed, shouted, "Well, F-U- too, Minerva," and hung up. We all laughed again shooing fear and disease away for a few precious minutes.

As other cousins made their "final call of respect" to visit Aunt Helen with chocolates she couldn't eat and flowers she couldn't smell, we would relive those times we all spent together on the farm in New Paltz. Our memories of life those summers on the farm were the medicine to ward off the inevitable death. The mention of the murder there was brought up over and over again, and each cousin had a different version. We could only agree that it was Philanthe's daughter who was murdered and that Philanthe had escaped the murderer's rampage by hiding in the farmhouse.

"Remember that scary tree?" my cousin asked as she brought the wet sponge lollipop to Aunt Helen's lips.

"I thought the murder took place in the barn. That place gave me the creeps," another cousin said as she picked dead flowers from the flower arrangement of red carnations. "Remember how the moms tried to keep us out of there?"

"Who was it, again, that was killed?" my sister asked.

"Philanthe's daughter, her two grandkids and Uncle Petros," I explained sounding like an authority, but not sure of my facts either.

"So that was Aunt Carrie's sister, right?" Kathy figured out. "Too bad we can't ask her. Aunt Carrie doesn't even know her own children. How can you forget your own kids?" Carrie was ninety and living in a nursing home. If she didn't have Alzheimer's, you can be sure she would have led a rebellion to get the hell out of there.

"Yes, but only Uncle Petros was killed at the farm. Philanthe watched him run up the field to the barn, and she hid under the bed." I added.

Strange, how that decrepit farmhouse that was the scene for a murder too unspeakable to talk about was the magnet that drew us all to New Paltz, the small college town that boasts such serene vistas of the Shawangunk Mountains. I went to college there. The aunts and uncles built homes and moved up there. When my mom died, my sister sought refuge there. She chose to select a house on the basis of its view of the mountains, the same mountains we adored because our parents valued them so.

We decided to ask Aunt Helen about Philanthe and the murder at the farm, but Helen could only whisper short phrases that might be replies to our question or to some dialogue in her delirious memory. "Your mom would know. That's right... gone."

Now what? How do we, the third generation find the answers when we were too busy to ask our mothers the right questions. When mom, Aunt Helen and Aunt Chris died, the torch was passed. Memories were locked in Aunt Carrie's mind. Suddenly the cousins were the only ones left to tell the story, and we never took time to ask the people who may have known. Hell, we didn't even know how we were related to each other. In our family, aunt and uncle were terms of respect, not necessarily relations. In truth, only Aunt Helen was my aunt; Christine and Carrie were cousins elevated to the status of "aunts" because of their age. All family members were double hugged and affectionately treasured.

That summer, living communally with three other families at the Spartan farmhouse in New Paltz, I got to meet my cousins, my aunts and the "Old Greeks" who came up to visit for the day. We were the youngest generation living a poor man's version of vacationing in the Catskills with four families, related to one another, under a very leaky roof of a farm that belonged to someone in the family.

The immigrants, the old Greeks, died off and became legends or caricatures; the Greek and Norwegian descent aunts became the matriarchs who framed us, and my third-generation American cousins became my lifelong friends. We were all so busy being the younger generation that we took for granted that as generations passed on so did the answers to those unasked questions, the questions the "old Greeks" could have answered.

When my Aunt Carrie developed Alzheimer's, we knew the answers were locked inside her. When my mom, who promised me she would live forever, died, there was still Aunt Helen who might remember. "Your mom would have known," Helen huskily whispered as she lay in a drug induced, pain-free Xanadu in the Mountain View Nursing Home, just five miles from the farmhouse and the barn that forged our ties in pubescent memories.

When my cousin Barbara brought Aunt Christine to visit and share our vigil, my sister asked, "Aunt Chris, tell us what you knew about the murder in the farmhouse."

"Don't ask me," explained Christine. "I'm the Norwegian side of the family, not Greek. I just knew there was a murder. Carrie's sister, I think." A few months later, she joined her best friends without knowing or caring about the secrets of the murder of Philanthe's brother, daughter, and two granddaughters.

Why did they not tell us about that horrible stabbing that took place in the barn? Maybe they did, but we did not listen.

Cemetery Reunion

Aunt Chris joined her husband, Goldie, in a grave that lay waiting for her for twenty-eight years. Moments after tossing flowers in Aunt Christine's grave, we cousins wandered over the grassy avenues of the New Paltz Rural Cemetery. We searched out familiar nooks in the tiny resting place at the foot of the Shawangunk Mountains. "Here's Aunt Helen and Uncle Joe." We paused and remembered and walked on down the dirt lane to the niches in the wall reserved for cremated ashes. "Here's mom," I called wishing that she had chosen to be with my father at Calverton rather than with her second husband, but New Paltz was the home to all those closest to her.

We circled the niche and silently faced the sun. There were a few collective tears but more smiles as we remembered the summers we all shared on the farm in New Paltz. Now they were all gone, all except Aunt Carrie who lingered without memory. In truth, she had gone before my mom, Aunt Helen and Aunt Chris. The uncles all died before the aunts. We walked, silently, to our parked cars and rode to the reception at Aunt Chris's house. There we would retell the stories that shaped our lives. We, the cousins, would ascend to our new roles. The matriarchs are all gone. They left us to remember and to wonder why they never told us about that awful murder in the farmhouse we all joyfully shared those summers when we were growing up.

Aunt Chris wanted to follow her friends to where there was no pain and no sorrow. She lasted seven months after Aunt Helen died. Aunt Helen hung on for fourteen months after her sister, my mom, died. They had shared eight decades together and were not happy to be separated. They had lived close to each other and moved from the happenstance of being born relatives to the selectivity of friendship. We imagined them clinking wine and beer glasses, reuniting with their husbands, in a heaven that erased all sickness and loneliness.

I bet they loved seeing all of their children, my cousins, sitting in the sun hosting the relatives who came to say good-bye to the last of the matriarchs. When the topic turned to the summers spent at the farm, as they always did, our heavenly parents probably had the answer to the question we cousins asked each other, "Why didn't they tell us about the awful murder in the family?" Their answer would be, "Why didn't you ask?"

The four celestial aunts, for Aunt Carrie will join them within the year, would turn to one another and conclude, "Why do they care so much about the murders of four people they did not know? Why dwell on the dead when they still have life and those they love? Why face the shadows when the sun shines for them?"

I picture them sitting cross-legged looking down and thinking, "Now it's their turn. I wonder if they can figure it out and earn the title of New Matriarchs," Aunt Helen would muse.

"Or patriarchs," Min would correct her older sister once more.

"That's right," Aunt Chris would once more agree. "We had sons too."

"Yes," Aunt Carrie would add. Her body still lingered on earth, but her mind hovered with the collective soul of her best friends and relatives. "We Greek women were strong."

"Norwegian women were strong too. We would just let our husbands think they were in control." Aunt Christine had the final word.

Aunt Carrie and
"The Long Good-bye"

Carrie sat in the faux-leather chair by the window of the nursing home. She felt a breeze even though the window was shut and barred with a wrought iron grill designed to look ornamental rather than its purpose to keep patients safely inside. She lifted the pink shawl that lay in her lap to her chin in response to the chill that wafted by and curled around her. How ironic--a pink shawl. Aunt Carrie never wore pink. She was not a pink kind of a lady. She was beige. She was khaki. She was black and gray. She was a black and white or sepia photograph captured without the excess of color. Patterns and prints were not a part of her wardrobe. Those bright colors would have wrestled with the woman who was colorful and bold enough without the window dressing of fabric.

This is the woman who toured Russia in the sixties when tourists were first let into the boundaries of this foreign land. This is the woman who packed her oldest clothes and discarded the soiled garment each day so she wasn't bogged down with luggage and laundry. Aunt Carrie was the real thing. She didn't carry a purse or wear jewelry. Such accessories would detract from her very solid self. She sure as hell wouldn't be sporting a pink, fringed shawl like the one she clutched to her face with both hands.

Alzheimer's disease had sucked the life out of her once animated face that, devoid of make-up, could be so expressive of her mood. She once had that Greek smile that was part of the Takis legacy; now the corners of her mouth were frozen in a lifeless pout. Only her eyes retained some of the intense, hazel-gold sparkle that once commanded a math class with the discipline of confidence.

She turned to the door when she heard it push into the room. Funny how the doors to hospitals and other institutions like this nursing home always open into, not out of, the room. Two men entered, and Aunt Carrie turned to face them by turning in her chair. She couldn't move too much because, under the pink shawl, another blanket was tucked so tightly to the chair that was wired to go off in the nurses' station if she decided to get up and wander off.

Her sons, Jimmy and Michael, walked to their mother and kissed her on the forehead.

"Company," Carrie thought. "The tall one reminds me of someone." Carrie's face softened remembering the feeling but not the fact that Jimmy looked so much like his father Bill. "Vassili." A name from the past flew past her mind like a moth about to be singed in a flame of consuming blaze of a misfired brain wave. Carrie would have been proud that Jim named his own son after his father. "Vassili." A shadow of the thought lingered and burned away.

"How are you today?" her younger son Michael asked. He lived and worked in the city so he was able to visit Aunt Carrie more often than Jimmy who lived in Michigan. Jim's administration spanned two colleges, and his work at Columbia brought him to New York every three weeks. The intermittent visits were like snap shots recording her abrupt decline. For Michael, visiting more often, the progressive loss softened and faded. It really didn't matter that Michael visited often. To Carrie, these men were as unknown to her as the orderly who came to change the linens on her hospital bed each morning.

Her sons each drew a chair close by their mother and held her hand chatting away about family, work, weather, news. It was a verbal ping-pong match with each man volleying conversation to each other in hopes that their mother might catch a part of it and react in some way with a knowing-expression or emotion.

Recently, after her ninetieth birthday celebration and months before Aunt Helen died, Carrie became silent. There were no messages given or received. The only response was the squeezing of the held hand. Whose hand was she was holding? Perhaps she was just holding on to this world while her mind had already escaped to a better place. Was there any memory or response to the immediate world?

When Jimmy and his wife, Gabriella, or when Jimmy and his brother Michael spoke of their mom's insular world, they pondered whether or not she was aware of them and her surroundings. They took comfort in seeing her respond to their mere presence. These visitors cared to spend time with her. The warmth of companionship flooded the dam of details held in some reservoir of her memory. She smiled at the men.

Esther, the nurse at the home, reassured the sons that Carrie would watch "The Honeymooners" on television and laugh. Surely there were parts of that once-brilliant mind that could remember. Maybe she was like a helpless baby bird in a shell that couldn't be broken from the inside out. Jimmy resisted the urge to take her, shake her violently, and yell, "I know you're in there. Come on out." Instead his brown eyes locked onto his younger brother's blue eyes. Without words and in a mirror image, they lowered their eyelids to half-mast and slowly looked away from each other to face their mother.

"Mom, would you like a glass of nice cold water?" Michael asked noticing that she was swiping her bottom lip with her tongue.

When he got no response, he poured a paper cup half full from the pitcher on the stand. She sipped from the straw brought to her lips.

"Cool and fresh," Carrie thought as her mind drifted to a kind place in her memory. She was at the family farm. It was summer. Her husband Bill would be driving up from Brooklyn tonight. Min just started the charcoal and Helen set the table. Aunt Chris made potato salad, and the girls husked the corn. It was almost time to call the little ones in for dinner. *"Jimmy, it's your turn to fill the pitcher with the water we got from the mountain spring."* Carrie was, once again, the woman in charge. *"Put it on the table on the porch. We're having hamburgers and hotdogs."* Carrie remembered, *"Nothing better than spring water on a hot July day."*

"Look, Jimmy." Michael noticed a hint of a smile. "Wonder what she's thinking." By the time her older son looked, the smile morphed into a frown of worry. She fretted and tugged at the all-too feminine blanket as she thought, *"The little ones didn't go in the barn, did they?"*

Discovery

After Aunt Christine joined Min and Helen, Aunt Carrie's passing became inevitable. It was like waiting for the last shoe to drop from the two pairs of comfortable Keds they wore on the farm that summer. We cousins were reconnected in the shared feeling of loss. Cards, calls and conversation all resurrected the time shared at the farm as children about to embark on independence. We all said the usual hollow promises like, "We need to get together. We can't just meet at weddings and funerals." The truth be told, we had each amassed families of our own, and that special time of being one big family for summer vacation was just a warm memory imprisoned in time but magnified by a multiple of ten as we each recounted silly things we said and did.

At each reunion we should have worn nametags to introduce our partners, spouses, children and grandchildren. We spoke of colleges and careers, trips and tragedy. As we spoke, we tossed information on a one-way journey to our cousins who, in turn, boomeranged similar statistics. All real conversations retreated to the farm and to the murder that we had since discovered in the New York Times article about how Philanthe had survived the murder of her younger brother Petros only to learn that her daughter Marika and grandchildren had already been slaughtered in Ozone Park. The Internet and libraries had recorded the awful truth. The details and facts were there for all to read. After the initial discovery, they became, for me, cold facts as impersonal as an episode of a TV murder mystery. Photos in tabloids could never be matched to the real people we knew. Someone, long ago, had purged Demi, Petros, Marika, Ann, and Helen from the family albums. Only Philanthe's portrait remains as a survivor who bore sadness like a burdensome pack on a pilgrimage.

Our mothers' lives, and now deaths, had been the magnetism that attracted the ten cousins. Like an Etch-A-Sketch toy, our iron filings always drew a similar picture. Anecdotes, distorted by time and perception, were shared, and our mothers became colorful cartoons, more comical and saintly than they probably were. Our bond was the summers at the farm. The one question we wanted to have answered is why we never knew about the murders. The answer was discovered in the life of Philanthe, a woman who, in spite of all hardships, kept going. She did not demand pity, nor did she bury her life in the coffins of her family. She went on. Our mothers, the next generation, did not wallow in the shadows of the past or bask in the notoriety of a family tragedy. They lived today with the gusto it deserved, knowing that the future comes to us moment by moment.

Philanthe's daughter Carrie, Philanthe's nieces Min and Helen, and Aunt Christine were the matriarchs that passed on that zest for life to my cousins and me. The memories of the summers on the farm in New Paltz were lessons about life, not death.

Graduation 1956

The Columbus Avenue School was right across the street from my home on Dehnhoff Avenue in Freeport, Long Island. The chain link fence had the entrance gate on the far side of the block. I was always late. I still am. I like to call myself an eleventh-hour person, when, in truth, I am eleven-fifty or later.

No one entered the school by the front entrance. We all walked around on the sidewalk to the playground and entered the back door. The front of the school was designed for visitors only with doors that opened out. They could only be pushed from the inside to allow guests into the auditorium. On graduation from sixth grade, students and parents proudly spilled out the front door to mull about in too-fancy clothes on the recently spiffed-up front lawn of the elementary school.

I remember wearing a pale, shiny dress in a color that was neither pink nor coral. It showed off my tan, my Greek heritage of olive skin that soaked up the sun without ever turning sunburned. The scoop neck would have shown cleavage if I had any to show. My padded bra, enhanced with a wad of Kleenex tissues, only gave the illusion of a blossoming chest that ended at a very flat upper chest. Its skirt ended at the knees even though I tried taping it shorter with scotch-tape.

I was hanging around with a group of best friends who were all talking about what they were going to do that summer. A few were off to summer camp. They were richer than I was.

Some were going to the summer recreation program where they would be herded from arts and crafts to some group sport or activity. Most were just going to hang out at Smitty's, the local candy store, play Canasta, and take the bus to Jones Beach. How I wished we were going to be home that summer to be with my friends. I longed to walk to the village to shop at Woolworth's or a bargain store we dubbed "Cheap Johns." We, at the age of twelve, had the freedom to walk the neighborhood, ride our bikes or the bus to spend time with friends from after breakfast to before supper.

Mom had waited until Graduation day to inform me that we and three other families were going to vacation at a farmhouse in New Paltz, New York.

"Where?" I asked.

"New Paltz," she answered. "It's an old farm that belongs to my father's family. You'll be there with your cousins."

"What cousins?" I wanted to know. I knew my Aunt Helen's kids were little. "I don't want to spend my summer vacation babysitting two little girls."

"Your cousin Kenny Gundersen will be there. He is the same age as you. In fact, he is just a few weeks older than you."

I knew Kenny Gundersen because we used to live a few houses away from him when we lived in Staten Island. What I remembered about him was that he had curly hair, was shorter than me, and that he was an annoying "tag-a-long." "You've got to be kidding. I can't spend four weeks with him. Aren't there any girls?"

"Well, no," mom countered, "but your cousin Jimmy will be there. He's a few months older than you. He's very much like you, actually. He is Aunt Carrie's son."

Aunt Carrie I remembered. She was a character and the kind of aunt you would want. She took me into Madison Square Garden once to see the circus. We were seated in the upper level and she called the peanut vendor over to our row. The man fell and twitched in the aisle next to us spilling peanuts in the aisle.

She tried to focus me on the trapeze act, but I kept staring at this poor man who wasn't moving. A crowd of staff workers surrounded this man and scooped him up and disappeared down the galley. Aunt Carrie took me to the sideshow even though she had just told me we couldn't go there because it wasn't right to make fun of people who were different. When she suddenly changed her mind, I knew the peanut man was dead. I hate the circus. She was right about the freaks. They made me sad. Circuses make me sad. I don't like peanuts either.

I wasn't sure I could survive a summer without my girlfriends. I was sure it would be dreadful, and I assumed the role of the martyr. My mood grew into a shell of selfishness, and I crawled into the abyss. I wet-blanketed the excitement my brother Kenny and sister Kathy had as they packed some toys. We each had a suitcase. Mine had make-up, curlers, and Evening in Paris perfume. I had vowed not to have fun, but, just in case, I wanted to look good.

Mom didn't break the news about the lack of plumbing and television until we were on our way up Route 17 and stopping at the Red Apple Rest. Even eating cheeseburgers washed down with chocolate malteds did not erase my victim's snit.

Four weeks in an old farmhouse in the middle of nowhere. I was being sent to a rural prison. I would have freaked out if I had known about the murder that took place there in the year that I was born—1944.

My grandparents

My grandparents, YiYia and Grandpa, came to visit us in Freeport, Long Island the weekend before we were to drive upstate to New Paltz in my father's station wagon, a behemoth of a car with wood panels on the side. This embarrassing vehicle would later be sought after by surfers and known as "a woody." At age twelve, everything made me self-conscious—my cape cod house with replica colonial furniture, the station wagon, my wardrobe, my family. I always wanted better, more expensive, and more stylish. Looking back, the things that shamed me are the things that I miss the most.

My grandparents came to visit on a Sunday. They always came on a Sunday. I'm sure they did something on Monday through Saturday, but I couldn't picture what their everyday life was like. To me they were held in suspended animation from one Sunday visit to the next one. They drove from Brooklyn to Long Island in a black sedan that sat idle the rest of the week. The entire visit would take place at the maple harvest table that belonged in a dining room but, since we did not have one, filled the kitchen. The table, leaves extended, had a glass top to prevent the everyday use to mar its surface. The chairs were on three sides with a maple bench slid under on the wall side. When company came, the table would be moved out from the wall leaving a narrow path for my mother to glide from the refrigerator to the stove past the sink and built in dishwasher. An EIK, the realtor's advertisement would call it-- an eat-in-kitchen.

Greeks talk over food. I am convinced that, in the absence of roast lamb and wine, there would be silence. So we surrounded the table and talked through dips and chips into the main meal, which usually consisted of leg of lamb, roasted vegetables, and salad with feta cheese and olives. Cheese and fruit followed the dessert and coffee. Dinner was more than a meal. Conversation concluded simultaneously with the dropping of the dinner napkin onto the plate.

YiYia had Parkinson's disease. She shuffled and shook, and her tongue would dart in and out of her juicy mouth like a swollen worm. She wore her white hair in a short bob parted in the middle. Naturally, she dressed in her black YiYia dress, the plain cotton button-up-the-front, short-sleeved dress that all Greek women wore as they got older. I used to call her shoes "witch shoes" because they laced up and were all pointy and misshaped from bunions and calluses. YiYia didn't say much. She was content to smile at us, and, once in a while, she would spontaneously hug us. Holding us captive, she might plant a slobbering kiss much like that of an exuberant puppy jumping face high to show affection. Shyly, she would release her bear hug grip, stand at arm's length, and just beam. I cruelly did not hug her back and would often use my sleeve to clean my face of her lingering wet kiss. How I wish I could pull her to me and now return her display of affection.

I found out years later that they think she developed Parkinson's from Encephalitis, the "Sleeping Sickness" she caught as a teenager in Gytheon, Greece. The foxy pictures of her as a young woman in the "roaring twenties" outfits with gobs of jewelry seemed like another person than the YiYia that I knew. She wore no earrings, necklace or bracelet. A single gold band adorned her left hand. Her jewelry was buried in a box in her dresser, a testimony to who she was, not who she became under the spell of palsy. Her daughters and grandchildren were her valuable gems that glistened in her hazel-green eyes.

My grandfather was corpulent. He was a big man, at least in my memory. He always wore a dark black or navy blue suit with a white shirt and a tie. Matching gold cufflinks held the laundry pressed sleeves. He wore a hat, winter and summer, and would lift it in a genteel greeting as he removed it entering the house.

I remember seeing him in short sleeves only once, and that was at the sandy creek beach in New Paltz. Everyone else wore a bathing suit, but he and YiYia sat at a picnic table in the shade, he in dress pants and white shirt, she in a rayon version of her black uniform. I never looked in their closets or drawers, but I could never picture them containing pajamas, nightgown or, heaven forbid, underwear. I would imagine their other clothes to be duplicates of what they now wore.

My grandfather, Aris, worked at Gregory's, the restaurant he and his brother Gregory owned in Brooklyn, and he was always bringing us some cooked lamb, buttery cookies called *Koulouri*a and Baklava. He was a fine cook and did all the cooking at home if he hadn't brought dinner home from the restaurant. After he died and YiYia lived with my aunt, I once saw her make soup, Campbell's chicken noodle. She struggled with the can opener, splashed the water as she added it to the concentrate, and shuffled in baby steps as she aimed a pot, held at arm's length with both hands on the handle, toward the stove. She turned and looked at me with pride.

At one time, in the teens and twenties, before the crash of 1929, my grandfather owned many restaurants, a hotel, and lots of real estate. He was a millionaire when a millionaire was someone who had lots and lots of money.

Grandpa didn't talk to us kids directly. He funneled conversation through the grown-ups as though we were speaking through a translator even though he spoke English perfectly. He knew the words, but the culture of the next generation was foreign to him. When he did speak to us, it was in a guided question and answer format.

"So, how are you doing at school? Do you have a boyfriend, a pretty girl like you?" he would ask me. To my mother he would say in Greek, "She looks just like Poppi, don't you think?" I would recognize the name Poppi. I knew she died before I was born. Everyone said I looked just like her. I sure hope she was pretty.

"And you, Kenny, you're getting so big. You'll be as tall as your dad some day."

Greeks have this thing about connecting one generation to another.

My sister would just get a pinch on the cheek and a smile. "So pretty. So light. Are you sure she is Greek?" and then he would laugh. "My little sister Philanthe had blue eyes, though. She was a blue-eyed Greek." My brother and sister were blond with blue eyes, like my Norwegian father. I had the dark hair, dark eyes, and olive skin of my mother. When I grew up, I promised myself I would dye my hair blonde. I never did.

After a meal that seemed like hours, and probably was over an hour, we children would be excused from the coffee and grown-up conversation that always ended the meal. We escaped the confines of the dining table like prisoners sprung from death row.

As I dashed out the door to go meet my friends in the schoolyard, I overheard Grandpa say to my mom and dad. "So you are going to the farm, I hear?"

"It's not such a nice place. Gone to seed, so to speak. Are you sure you don't mind roughing it?"

"It'll be fun with all the four families sharing the work. It'll give the kids something to do and enjoy the country," Mom assured him.

My YiYia clucked and shook her head. "No so good."

"It'll be fine. The kids'll enjoy the adventure of it."

"Don't tell them."

"Don't tell them what?"

"You know. Don't tell them about what happened there."

"I won't, mom. They didn't even know Petros or the others."

My grandfather raised his hand in a signal a dog trainer would use to signify "Stay." Conversation ceased as the four adults looked from person to person. My dad looked confused.

"No more!" My grandfather tensed and cast his eyes toward the dessert plate still sticky with the baklava honey.

When he looked up, his face was once again animated and softened. As the conversation changed to small talk, a memory was buried deeper in his past. Returning to the present, he asked, "So, Carol goes to Freeport Junior High School next year. Are you ready to have a teenager in the house?"

Glad to have the mood broken and the topic changed, mom answered, "She is already on the phone constantly. She is giving me a hard time about leaving her friends for a month."

Thirteen years earlier, another "almost teenager" felt the same way about going to the farm with her family.

Just before Easter in 1943, Ann and her younger sister Helen, called "Eleni" by her Greek name, complained about leaving their friends to spend their week's vacation in New Paltz with their Uncle Petros. Ann was almost thirteen and would rather stay in the city. Her mother Marika pleaded with her, "Please understand, honey. Your YiYia will be there all week, and your dad will come up to the country on the weekend. We'll have fresh eggs to dye red, and Uncle Petros thinks he can find us lamb for Easter dinner."

"But we can have red eggs and lamb here," Ann countered.

"Yes, I know, but a week in the country will be such a nice change. Uncle Gregory and Aunt Georgia will be there on Sunday."

"Who cares?"

"*I do, honey. I don't get to see my aunts and uncles that much.*"

"*Daddy doesn't want to go either. He said he wants to spend Easter with just us, here, at home.*"

Easter 1943

Marika and the girls ran up the staircase with suitcases in hand. They turned right into the largest bedroom in the farmhouse. The long room had both a double and a single bed. Ann claimed the single bed closest to the road. Marika liked this room best because it had the most windows. You could see the front and side of the house at the same time. She and Helen would share the double bed.

Her mother, Philanthe, would use the adjoining small bedroom that faced the barn. Philanthe loved how the sun would pour in the tall windows in the morning. She savored the presence of her daughter and granddaughters in the room next door. Even though the door could close making two separate rooms, the three generations chose to sleep dormitory style.

If Demi joined them, he would choose the bedroom down the hall, past the attic stairs.

"Mom, should I put my valise under the bed or in the closet?" Ann asked.

"Under the bed, dear. Out of the way," Marika answered. "Then come down so we can have lunch on the porch. It can be our indoor picnic."

"Where's Helen?" Ann wanted to make sure her little sister wasn't doing something more fun than she.

"Helen is out collecting eggs with Uncle Petros. After lunch we can boil them and dye them with the red food coloring I brought."

The Four Families Who Summered
At The Farmhouse In New Paltz

Minerva (nee Takis 1921) and Olaf Kenneth Olsen
      Carol (1944)
      Kenny (1947)
      Kathy (1948)

Helen (nee Takis 1916) and Joseph Vecchione
      Jane (1952)
      Elaine (1955)

Carrie (nee Kontolefa 1917) and Vassilis (Bill) Jacobs
      Jimmy (1944)
      Michael (1955)

Christine (nee Hansen 1922) and Golman Gundersen
      Kenny (1944)
      Barbara (1949)
      Gary (1955)

The Farmhouse
Summer of 1956

If all four families were there, as they were in the summer of 1956 when I was twelve, our vacation at the farm was run like a matriarchal summer camp with Aunt Carrie, Philanthe's daughter as its commandant. The old farmhouse was spacious and rambling with its five bedrooms, large living room, separate dining room, front porch and typical farm kitchen complete with a wood-burning enameled stove along with a more modern gas range.

The four families combined four female adults, three teenagers, six little ones, and my brother Kenny who at eight, like a Euglena, was sometimes a big kid and other times one of the little ones. Out of the teenagers, I was the only girl, and since I had just gotten my period that spring, I had royal status of being included, sometimes, with the women, with whom I shared pubic hair, boobs, and hormonal moods. On the weekends, the fathers would come up. Life changed when the men were "visiting" the house. The unity of the aunts and cousins was mathematically divided into four family units that worked independently, rather than as a mass.

We teenagers, or almost teenagers, were cousins just months apart in age. This cohort became my posse. We considered ourselves separate from the rest of the kids. We operated in what we thought was independence from the mothers and from the little ones. Looking back, we were still under the watchful eye of the mothers who, in turn, did the bidding of Aunt Carrie.

Each family took a room upstairs, and the downstairs bedroom was saved. No one slept in there. It was just empty with its bed and dresser. This bedroom was off the kitchen. It had two doors, one to the kitchen and another to the living room, and two windows that faced the barn and the outhouse. It was a strange room in a farmhouse. Perhaps it was originally for a hired hand or cook. It was not particularly suitable to be a bedroom with four exits and hardly any space to position the old iron bed with a creamy chenille bedspread and the dark mahogany vanity dresser. There was a plastic antimacassar on the dresser top with a small milk-glass dish that held two mismatched buttons and a paperclip. The mirror was foggy, but it reflected the morning sun from the window on the opposite wall. Thinking back, I see the irony of fourteen of us cramped into the rest of the house leaving this room as a shrine to "someone who might need it." This room belonged to Petros, Philanthe's brother, who was murdered a dozen years before. No one mentioned that fact.

My teenage boy cousins and my brother Kenny bunked out in the living room. This large room was filled with lumps of sleeping bags, couches and pillowcases filled with tee shirts and shorts. The room was always dark because the porch, which must have been added later, blocked the windows that would have faced the front of the house, the side with that huge old maple tree across the road. No one went into that room except the three boys. Besides, it smelled like dirty socks and musty pillows from the scratchy couch that sat so low to the floor that you had to fall backwards onto it and be fork lifted out of it. The living room had the uninviting aura of the least popular frat house.

The four ladies, my mom and aunts, divided up the four upstairs bedrooms. Mom had the largest room with the most windows. One window looked out over the porch to the magnificent shade tree across the road. The other two windows looked out over what must have been a garden before the Queens Anne's Lace and Black-Eyed Susans claimed it as home. The room had two beds, both cream-colored iron in the shape of rounded ladders as headboards and footboards.

"Cool. I'll take this single bed by the window that faces the road," I declared, lacking the grown-up logic that it would have made more sense for me to share the double bed with my little sister and let my mom, Min, have the single bed. Kathy was four years younger and had no objections to the rare opportunity to cuddle up to mom as they slept like back to back commas in the full bed just one foot away from mine. "It's like the one I'll have someday in my home, except mine will be shiny brass with a down comforter and lots of lacy pillows." I had seen the bed in the Montgomery Ward catalogue and added it to my list of "I Wants" that was getting longer every day. Thinking back, I was the only person there with my own bed. Everyone else shared.

I staked my claim by putting my clothes, mostly short-shorts and sleeveless tee shirts into one drawer of the only dresser in the room. It was empty. On the top stood one old alarm clock with its arms stuck at 9:16. I shoved my Samsonite blue suitcase under the bed.

"Mom, there's another suitcase under here," I complained as I tried to stuff mine under the bed. I noticed how low the bed was to the floor then figured out that it had no box spring, just a wire frame.

"Leave it alone. It doesn't belong to you," my mom reprimanded.

"But there might be something really cool inside. Come look."

"I said, 'Leave it under there.' It is not yours. We're guests here."

"Okay," I replied knowing full well that my cousins and I would sneak up here later and investigate the treasure. We loved exploring the old farmhouse, but there were some places that even we were cautious in investigating.

"Okay, mom. I'll just put my suitcase in the corner."

When my cousins and I snuck back into the room while everyone was outside, we looked under my bed. We were convinced there had to be something valuable in that suitcase. Why would it be there otherwise? All three of us got down on all fours and had to lean on our chests to see underneath.

"It's gone." I said disappointedly. "Oh, well. It was probably empty anyway." I was getting good at this sour-grapes thing. "My mom must have moved it to put my suitcase under there."

I loved that bed. It was my safety zone. I would sleep later than the mothers and the little ones, and in the early morning, I could hear the symphony of children and women's voices as the day began with grooming and breakfast. Deeper, raspy, morning laughter came from the boys' dorm that was beneath our bedroom. As I lay in the old iron bed, I would sometimes stretch my arms above my head and grab on to the iron spindles that still felt cold from the night air. They were the circumferences of a man's penis, but at age twelve, I had yet to see one in real life. I had often searched to get a real clear look at that taboo body part in those French books that were in my father's top drawer at home in Long Island. "Sort of goofy looking," I thought. "I can't imagine having that stuff hanging between my legs. Doesn't it get in the way?"

Those mornings, waking to the sunlight as it made a visible swath in the dust particles, were my awaking to that grown-up world of sex and love. I, virginal and curious, felt the longings and the curiosity of sex. I knew how you did it. I had heard enough dirty jokes and read enough love novels, but it didn't all make sense. I had used a tampon, so I knew where that penis was supposed to go, but inserting a cardboard cylinder was uncomfortable, not pleasurable. Maybe sex is only pleasurable for men. I would touch myself and felt tingly. "Something like the cross between a tickle and a sneeze" was the way the pamphlet described an orgasm. "Not much to look forward to," I thought. Mom, always avoiding the uncomfortable subject, had given me the pamphlet when I got my period before she had a chance to have that mother to daughter chat with me. Of course, I knew all about it. That's what girlfriends are for.

I would loll in my bed and wait until the one bathroom was vacant and, selfishly, I knew that the buckets of water would be replenished so I could flush. Toilet bucket brigade was the job of the little ones who liked to play with the outside pump. The mothers would lug the heavy, filled buckets upstairs. The rule was to flush "only if you did something 'important.'" Since I considered everything I did as special and important, I always flushed. Like a princess, I would make a grand entrance, completely dressed with my invisible tiara, as I strolled down the staircase to the dining room.

There I became the protégé of the ladies. After all, I was almost a lady, almost a grown-up. I was twelve, in junior high school, and I had had my period twice already.

That summer of 1956, the four ladies seemed very old to me. Now I am thirty years older than they were that summer. My god, they were in their mid to late thirties.

The aunts weren't all related to each other, but they all were related to my mom. Min was the common denominator to the aunts. Helen was mom's sister, and Aunt Carrie was mom's cousin. They were all Greek, but born in America. Aunt Christine was really my father's cousin. She was Norwegian and was blonde, feminine and timid in comparison to the dark, confident Greek women. I wonder if she felt strange immersed in this culture of Greek relatives, customs and food. If she did, she said nothing. In fact, Aunt Chris wouldn't say anything if she had a mouth full of "you-know-what."

Aunt Christine's room was the only room that was marginally decorated. A comb, brush and mirror were carefully placed on a lace doily on the bureau. I remember the bottle of

Avon Timeless on her dresser and the fragrance of hair spray on her hair. Aunt Chris actually set her hair in curlers. She was the one aunt who ironed blouses and could look dainty and feminine in her jeans, which were called dungarees back then.

Aunt Helen had naturally curly hair and always wore shorts and a tee shirt. I remember the shorts because you could see the scars from the car accident. Aunt Helen was short and looked even shorter because her legs seemed crooked making her appear closer to the ground. Maybe Philanthe wasn't the only one who was a tad superstitious. Helen and Min's mother, my *YiYia*, was clairvoyant. When Helen had her accident, Helen was working for the War Department in Washington, D.C. My *YiYia* was in Brooklyn. In the middle of the night, she roused my grandfather, Aristomenes, and my mother and said, "*Ella, Ella.* Come. Come. Helen is hurt." Without a phone call, they headed for D.C. and went from hospital to hospital until they found her in a coma. Another time, when Helen and Min were young, they were sitting in the Rolls Royce (did I ever mention that my grandfather was rich?) with the chauffeur Ben. In Greek, *YiYia* screamed as she grabbed them and pulled them out of the car, "No. No. *Ella.* Get out of the car." In a panic, she unfortunately screamed in Greek, and the girls responded to her commands. Ben didn't. In a moment, the car caught fire and exploded burning Ben badly. The two little girls were not burned. I think Greeks have cornered the marked on ESP. Helen was the survivor. She quietly and stoically overcame explosions, disease, accidents and acne. She wasn't pretty, but you forgot that when you realized how truly nice she was. She got prettier the more you knew her. She had married my Uncle Joe and had her first baby at forty. Since she had an infant and a toddler, she took the bedroom that you entered through our bedroom.

Min, short for Minerva, was my mom and Helen's sister. She was taller and had softer features than Helen. I think you would call my mother attractive because she was pleasant looking and had a great shape. She rarely showed it off except in a bathing suit. She was most comfortable in jeans or denim Bermuda shorts. Her hair was short and full of cowlicks. Probably what made her seem more attractive than she was had to do with the fact that she smiled most of the time. She was one of the smiling Greeks. She was blessed by inheriting that genuine love of life. All was good. All was okay. If life gave you lemons, mom would make Whiskey Sours and throw a party. People liked to bask in her smile.

Carrie was Philanthe's daughter. Carrie was the most natural of all the women. She was a bit plump and wore shorts and tops that were loose and sloppy looking. In fact, one summer she was pregnant, and her clothes remained the same. Her wardrobe was shades of khaki, beige, and drab green. The fashion police would have incarcerated her for her bathing suit. The elastic had long since left it, and her boobs were free to hang even lower than they did when they were contained in her less than eighteen-hour bra. She had inherited the weak stomach muscles of her mother Philanthe. Besides, Carrie wouldn't have bothered to suck in her gut for fashion's sake.

Aunt Carrie's hair was even more unruly than Min's. She had visible bumps on her head (She called them brain bumps) that made some shocks of hair stand up rather than lie down as she combed it. Carrie was the most independent of these strong women. She had dropped out of high school to take a job to help support her family. Another version had her kicked out for smoking because, back then, everyone smoked, so I doubt that ended her high school career. More likely she wanted to help out her widowed mother and younger brother. Carrie read voraciously and frequented museums and concerts with a passion. She married Bill who was much older than she was. When Jimmy, her son and my cousin, was in high school, she decided to get her GED since Jimmy excelled at Peter Stuyvesant High School and was destined to become a college president. Carrie passed the test with such flying colors that the proctor suggested she try the College Proficiency. She qualified for two years, so she went right from dropout to sophomore in College. Once she became a student, she kept going until she got her Masters and taught mathematics at a private academy which enabled Michael, her youngest son, to attend school there.

Carrie had a love of learning. Her name was the muse of music and epics, but I believe that she was misnamed. She should have been Clio, the muse of history. She couldn't carry a tune, but she devoured literature. Carrie was raw power. She was a "no crap" lady who could hold her own with any man, any woman, anytime and anyplace. She was, after all, Philanthe's daughter.

More than family, these four ladies were friends. That enabled all of us cousins to become friends too. The summers at the farmhouse were filled with sunshine, joy and love. I am glad they never told us about the murder in the barn.

The Barn

"I wish you three wouldn't go up to the barn with the younger ones," Aunt Carrie pleaded with her son Jimmy. "You, Kenny and Carol are older, but the little ones will follow you. You know that."

It didn't seem like a problem to us. We cousins were all twelve years old when we first explored the deserted barn that was on the Takis farm property. The farm had been in the family since the thirties. Petros, who was still a bachelor at forty-five, bought the farm and, during the war, lived in it while he worked in a defense plant in Poughkeepsie. It was his home and haven for his brothers and sisters and their families since they all lived in the city.

Young Peter Kontolefa, Philanthe's son, had been asthmatic and anemic. Philanthe, herself, harbored tuberculosis in her lungs. Doctors said it would be good for the young boy and his mother to breathe some clean, country air. He was probably our age when he first came to New Paltz to stay with his family. The rest of the brothers and sisters of Philanthe inherited the Spartan farmhouse after Petros was killed. Not knowing what to do with it with so many shared owners, it stood empty most of the time. Spiders and ghosts lived there full-time; Greek relatives would visit the farmhouse on weekends and summers. No one stayed very long. Now twenty years later, Philanthe's grandson, Jimmy, and his cousins spent summers on the farm. They breathed life back into the stagnant air of the murder scene.

The farmhouse was the first house on Hasbrouck Road. On the right side of the road that curved around to other small farms were fields and a magnificent view of the Shawangunk Mountains. On the left side on the almost forty-five degree curve sat the old farm. The house could be called a saltbox, and it might have had some white paint on it at some time. Now, in the mid fifties, it looked drab, a color not readily defined as tan or gray. The roof had, perhaps, been black, but was now faded and bleached to a dirty gray. There was no trim, so the windows didn't stand out. Unwashed, they were dingy and streaked and blended into the siding.

There was no running water the first summer we spent there. There was a hand pump just outside the kitchen door, and the chore of drawing water was either a bother or a joy, depending on the age of the child. There was always an empty five-pound can of Maxwell House Coffee by the pump. It was to be kept full of water at all times. The water would be used to prime the pump. We quickly mastered the technique of pouring the water from the can slowly into the hole by the handle as another cousin pumped slowly, then steadily, and the third cousin would man the buckets. Then we would proudly carry, careful not to spill any the precious liquid, into the kitchen. We repeated the process once again, and those two buckets were carried into the kitchen, through the large room we used as a communal dining hall, and up the flight of stairs to the bathroom that was at the top of the stairs. There was a toilet, a sink and a claw-footed bathtub. Nothing worked. The buckets of water were for the ladies, our four mothers, who would flush any accumulation of nighttime pee and morning poop. We kids were instructed to pee in the bushes or use the outhouse. For this bodily function, I was considered one of the ladies. It was one of the few times in my life that I actually enjoyed being a menstruating woman.

The "no water/no plumbing" inconvenience only lasted the first summer. We were Brooklyn, Staten Island and Long Island families used to more conveniences. In fact, at home I had my own bathroom attached to my upstairs bedroom in our Cape Cod home in suburbia. We roughed it that first summer, and then my father and Uncle Goldie went to work on improvements. One summer with no functional plumbing was enough of an adventure. The mothers: my mom Min, my aunt Helen, my aunt Carrie, and my aunt Christine were still young wives who wanted a warm bath before their husbands would come up on the weekend. I often wondered how they ever managed lovemaking. Perhaps they did, but we kids were so wrapped up in our own lives that our parents became invisible unless they were feeding us or driving us somewhere.

A few miles up the mountain road was the Brauhaus Restaurant. At least twice a week we children would be treated to a hamburger, fries and a Coke. We would be systematically dismissed from the tables to go to the bathroom and use the warm water to wash our face, hands, and any other body part that was not hygienic from the lukewarm daily scrub. We each carried toothbrushes in our jean pockets and passed the toothpaste to the next cousin at his or her turn.

Actually, we bathed daily in the swimming hole. If it wasn't raining, we spent our days at a place in Tillson that had a sandy shore, a bathhouse, and an ice cream wagon that did a lively business from the cousins. At age twelve, the width of the river seemed an impossible distance from shore to shore. By our fourth summer, we teenagers would swim to the far shore and chase the horses that had come to drink the running water.

Ivory soap was passed around to make sure all those parts under the bathing suit got special attention. We would bring clean clothes and change in the bathhouse.

These ladies were resourceful as they cooperatively ran the farm as a camp for their families. Money went into the "kitty" which was another empty Maxwell House Coffee Can. They would shop at the supermarket and at farm stands on their shopping trips. One or two of the mothers and a few chosen children would drive to town for provisions. Usually there would be one station wagon or Aunt Carrie's old Nash Rambler left while the husbands carpooled back to their city jobs. The moms took turns cooking and setting the table and cleaning up.

Even though we called it the farm, not a thing grew there. No one sowed, planted, pruned or harvested. There were a few apple trees that had grown too tall and wild to produce really good apples. The commercial apple orchard was within stealing distance. It was adjacent to the farm, and as we got braver, we investigated the area "beyond the barn."

I am sure our mothers kept an eye on us, but they were busy with the younger ones. Jimmy, Kenny G. and I, the almost-teenagers, and sometimes my brother Kenny were allowed to just "play." My brother was sometimes lumped into the younger or older category depending upon the situation. It was confusing having two cousins named Kenny, so my poor little brother got dubbed "Baby Kenny or Little Kenny." It got really confusing since my father used his middle name, Kenny, shunning his too ethnic Norwegian name, Olaf. A total of three people were named Kenny.

Usually it was harder to keep track of the Greek names. The first son is named after his patriarchal grandfather, and the first daughter is named after the patriarchal grandmother (YiYia). In one family with many children, there might be multiple Georges, Peters, or Nicks.

No matter the name or the relation, we were all dismissed summarily with, "Go out and play. Be careful and come back for lunch. After lunch we will go swimming." These were the instructions delivered by one of the moms, usually Aunt Carrie. We used to call her the Sergeant. She would bark orders and no one would dare talk back or plead for leniency.

Aunt Carrie was born here shortly after Philanthe came to America with her two older daughters, Libby and Marika. Carrie was Americanized for Kalliope. There is no C in the Greek alphabet, so her name and mine, Carol, became K in translation to Greek. Her name, like her grandmother's, meant "beautiful music" like a calliope or merry-go-round. Music, my ass! Her voice was gurgly. It slid up and down the scale like a bad song. Each note was definitive, and Carrie didn't mince words. She was used to being obeyed.

Her husband Bill was considerably older, and he deferred to her wishes. Her sons Jimmy and Michael followed her commands as though they were cubs, and she the sow bear.

Carrie bossed the other women too. Well, bossed is too strong a word. She commanded, she directed, she led the troops. She was not the oldest. Aunt Helen was a year older, but Helen was definitely the soft follower who said, "Sure. Whatever you say. Whatever you think. That will be fine with me."

Actually, with four families and ten children, we needed Aunt Carrie to make those decisions. Yes, that is what she was. She was the decision maker. She was definitely an enlightened despot who ruled the farmhouse. Min might discuss or temper the decision, but Christine and Helen were the sheep who followed. Aunt Carrie ruled this rag-tag kingdom of summer vacation.

Given the command to "Go out and play," we older ones would head off in our safety zone of about two thousand feet from the farmhouse. If we followed the road, we came to the brook and the hay field, and if we were lucky, we might see the neighbor's goats and feed them grass. If we crossed the road, we found ourselves in a meadow with brushy trees that we would climb in or make forts. When the farm was a working farm, this field was probably a hay field. Left uncut for a decade or more, only one maple tree grew tall and dominated the road and meadow with its huge shadow. As we got older, we would just create an adult-free zone to talk and hang out. Sometimes we would smoke Winstons and Marlboros that we would sneak out of Carrie or Min's packs.

Mostly, we headed to the barn. It was old and worn with some of the siding exposing sunlight. Its metal roof was no longer shiny or silvery. It was streaked with rivulets of rust giving it a coppery-gray hue that had just enough sheen left to reflect sunlight or moonlight.

The windows were gone, or, perhaps, it never had them. You could tell the part where animals were once kept, but the stanchions were gone and the hay and feed picked clean by decades of mice and chipmunks. Some feathers remained, and we stuck them in our hair pretending to be Indians. Aunt Chris gave us a lecture about getting lice, and Aunt Carrie looked at the chicken feathers and scowled. She never mentioned that her Uncle Petros had a thriving chicken farm here before World War II. We probably wouldn't have cared about the family history lesson anyway. I didn't know any Uncle Petros.

There was a water pump there, and sometimes, since we now knew the technique of priming, we would get it to gush out some frigid water, which was tinged with rust, from some ancient well.

There was also a small room in the barn that was partitioned off that held an old desk. Perhaps the farmer sat here to record sales of livestock or purchased supplies. Dusty and splintered, it held a treasure trove of keys. Skeleton keys we called them, and we would sort them and resort them and then place them back in the left hand top drawer where they were found. The desk itself had a keyhole in its top drawer above the kneehole, but none of the keys fit it.

The barn also had a loft that had collapsed through the supporting timbers. No real floor to walk upon, and there was no ladder attached to reach that height. At the time, it never occurred to me that there was no debris from that fallen loft on the floor or the barn. In fact, the barn stood there very neatly devoid from all extraneous junk or lumber. It was the modern equivalent of the Parthenon. It stood on the hill, an agrarian acropolis, as the bones of a building that once held animals and people and life and death. Especially death, but we didn't know that as almost-teenagers. Only Aunt Carrie knew for sure. Perhaps Min, my mom, and her sister Helen knew about the murders, but only Aunt Carrie experienced the event of the barn's awful secret. After all, it was her uncle, her sister, and her nieces.

Maybe Aunt Helen knew more, but she would protect us. Maybe that is why her children never were allowed in the barn. Aunt Chris knew nothing, I am sure. Aunt Chris surrounded herself with innocence and naiveté. Only the safe, the secure, the pretty and the nice were allowed in her world. The murder in the barn was none of those.

The Barn 1943

"Mother, Ann and I are going up to the barn with Theo."

"Okay, but change into your old shoes. The field is still wet with morning dew."

"Oh, mother, it's dry enough. Theo has a path cut with the mower going right from the kitchen door to the barn door." Ann countered. The path was two or three swaths of the push mower kept low as the rest of the grass grew up to hay. At one time, Petros had a flourishing chicken farm and used the hay to line the hen boxes. He still kept a few chickens for his own use and company. Chickens pretty much tended themselves. He would leave the barn door open during the day when he drove to work, but would shut the heavy sliding door at night when weasels and raccoons would stalk plump chickens.

Ann and Helen loved gathering the eggs from the nests and carried them back to the kitchen so proudly you would think they had laid them themselves.

What Ann and Helen loved best about the barn was the barn itself. Once, when their cousins John, Tina and Billy were visiting, they played hide and seek in the stanchions and in the little side stalls. Helen remembered hiding under the old desk for so long that she finally yelled out, "I'm in here." The five cousins came running to her, and, in the courage of numbers, they investigated the old kneehole desk that held treasures of broken pencils, old keys, and a cigar box full of odd screws and nails and such. The skinny top drawer was locked, a fact that led to youthful speculation of treasure and booty.

The youngsters could never understand why the barn was off limits to them unless they were "supervised." It was pretty far from the house, nearly five hundred feet. It was far enough to represent independence from the grown-ups. To them a barn was work or a chore. To children it was a forbidden playground.

Three Dog Days

There were three dogs that spent weekends with us that August on the farm. Dolly, Skippy and Tippy provided the twelve feet and three tales that milled in and out the screen door, slept on the green lawn, and hovered under the picnic table hoping for scraps. I think they must have gone home with the fathers because I can't recall being responsible for them as the week unfolded, but they always seemed to be there in snapshots with their alpha masters.

Our dog, Dolly, was a Springer Spaniel and some other canine that happened by in the neighborhood. I can still picture her emerging from the river at Midway Park with her tail waving like a flag of surrender. The tip of her tail had been cropped, but the long white hair continued to grow.

Jimmy's dog, Skippy, was the city dog that lived in an apartment on St. James Street in Brooklyn. A raw carrot dangled above his nose would provide a circus performance of leaps, jumps, and pirouettes. His weekend in the country and ride in the car with Carrie's Bill must have seemed like doggie-heaven on earth: real grass to pee in, no leash, and endless pats on the head. Skippy was a black and white something or other with pointy ears and tail and short, city-proper, fur.

The Gundersen's mutt was Tippy, so named because only the tip of his tail, which stood straight up like an exclamation point, was white. Otherwise, he was brown with short legs and a sturdy body that was so stubby that when he waved his tail, his whole body did internal turns that set off a series of stadium waves. Uncle Goldie, Christine's husband, taught Tippy to balance on an inner tube, and the pup would stand there frozen stiff floating around us until one of us tipped him over. Perhaps that was another reason for his name. We would, of course, scoop him up and place him back on the tube. He was the only dog small enough to be picked up. I think he was part Dauschund, but instead of being long, he looked like a closed accordion.

No pure breeds for us. We, like the dogs, were mixes of nationalities and places. Long Island, Staten Island, and Brooklyn were lost in the summer of exploring nature unlike our home surroundings. It was as if Mother Nature said to us, "Let's play. I've got toys and games enough for everyone."

Unlike today's youth who need batteries or electricity to function, we brought very little to the farm to amuse ourselves. I packed a record player that was the size of a foot square suitcase. It resembled a suitcase with its clasp and red, fake-leather, paper covering. It played 78 and 33 rpm records unless you stuck one of those black plastic disks into a 45 record. We had about a dozen records that were played over and over, and we sang "The Great Pretender" by the Platters in blissful cacophony like tone-deaf karaoke singers. I brought a writing pad and pencil; Jimmy had his collection of baseball cards and a few books. Kenny G brought a whiffle bat and ball. Mostly we discovered the bountiful supply of entertainment that imagination and the environment provided.

Rocks were painted with the purple ink of poison-berry bushes. A dandelion made a fine paint brush that spread as much indigo on the rock as it did on our hands. Sanctuaries were made out of sumac trees whose branches were easy to break and pile up into fortress like mounds. Daisies could be plucked until you got the desired result of "He loves me." Thick grass could be placed between two thumbs to make a reed that, when blown through, made a shrill, annoying noise guaranteed to make someone yell, "Will you please cut that out!"

The stream that was just around the bend held aquatic treasures. Catching crayfish and little baby fish in kitchen strainers and pails provided hours of fun and challenge as we tight-rope-walked on fallen logs and danced across slippery rocks trying not to, but secretly hoping to, fall in the cool, fresh brook water. Sneakers back then came in two colors: Girls wore plain, white Keds; boys wore black, Converse, ankle-length, basketball sneakers. We had our "Creek Sneaks" and our newer, hopefully dry, versions at home.

The apple and Damson plum trees were our tree houses and our sustenance. The apples were still green and the plums rock-hard, but they were the forbidden fruit of our teenage years, and, oh, they tasted so good.

Spontaneous games would erupt. A smack on the back would initiate a foot race or game of tag. An apple hit with a badminton racket would evolve into a freakish game of applesauce tennis using the clothesline at the net. A tennis ball was magical. It could be "Pickle in the Middle" or coupled with a stick a game of baseball with kitchen sponges as bases and a broomstick as a bat. If a piece of level ground could be found, a tennis ball could be bounced forever in a game of "A my name is Anne, and my husband's name is Andy. We come from Arizona, and we buy apples."

Bugs were our fascination. Some unwritten treaty of mercy protected a Praying Mantis and a Stick Bug, but others were fair game. At night we would catch lightening bugs and place them in jars with the metal lid punctured with small air holes. They became our mystical lanterns at night but gruesome bug tombs by morning. Japanese beetles were collected like a bounty. Jars with crawly bugs and their leaves would line the small cement step outside the kitchen screen door.

Kathy and Barbara and sometimes Jane would provide the moms with a daily bouquet of fresh wild flowers. To a child, a flower and a weed are the same. When do we lose that love of all things pretty and begin to differentiate between the valuable and the disposable? A mason jar, arranged with daisies, Queen Anne's Lace, Black-eyed Susans, Joe-Pye Weed, and Golden Rod, became the picnic table's centerpiece.

Our favorite game was just exploring. We never were quite brave enough to go up in the farmhouse attic, but we could spend an entire morning searching the old barn for hidden treasure. There were dark places, like the cow and pig trough, contrasted by light that slanted into the old barn from the windowless windows and from the sliding weathered barn door rusted eternally open on its overhead slide rail.

A chicken feather, a stray coin, wisps of straw, an old key or a broken farm implement could be the inspiration for a supposition. I wonder what the barn was like with animal noises and smells? Now it was lifeless, dusty, and stagnant. Only the deserted, mud packed nests of barn swallows on the rafters reminded us that this was once a place of throbbing life. To break the stifling silence, someone would say, "You're it. Count to fifty." And the rest of us would hide in the nooks and crannies of the barn.

Four O'clock in the Afternoon

At four o'clock the August sun would slant and soften and head toward the mountain. Whoever placed the farmhouse on those fifty some acres must have studied the rising and falling of the sun to place the front porch, which held the front door that no one used, to face the road and across to the field in the direction of the light traveling to its night resting place on the other side of the mountain. The house, placed too close to the curve in the road, was situated in such a way that a stranger might not know how to enter. The screen door to the porch held no lock, and the front door had no bell. The formal entry led to a dining room that was used as a hallway except for rare moments that the whole slew of us might eat at the huge table. Breakfast was eaten in shifts of age groups in the kitchen and dining room; lunch was a picnic somewhere, and dinner, really supper, was always on the screened porch in two sittings. As the day unfolded, the focus of activity moved from one end of the house to the other. We followed the sun like photo-topic life forms.

That mountain, with its distinct hump upon which the Mohonk Resort rises like Rapunzel's tower, and its famous "gunks," rocky cliffs that define the Shawangunk ridge, is the modern realtor's dream. The view would add a few hundred thousand to the asking price of properties in years to come. The small village of New Paltz, the college and most of the suburban houses all look up at a vista that is so perfectly composed that one would think an artist concocted its profile and palette. Looking back, I realize that the farmhouse was prime real estate. It's not that we did not value the shabby farmhouse. We simple noticed its vista without putting a price on it. As we ate dinner on the screened porch, we could trace the path of the sun as the gnarled tree we feared obliterated it. Miraculously it reappeared, illuminating the ochre fields of the hill my father called "God's little acre." Once it reached the rocky zenith, it seemed to speed up and then disappear suddenly. Night, in August, on our side of the mountain, came earlier. Dusk appeared the minute the last of the paper plates and serving dishes disappeared from the picnic table.

The four o'clock sun would pause in its journey. It would seem to stand still, and the hour between four and five was the best time of everyone's day. We blossomed like those blood red flowers called Four O'clocks that grew behind the house. We couldn't see them unless we rounded the corner to the overgrown side of the house. At one time Uncle Petros grew his victory garden with bright flowers haphazardly planted among the vegetables. Now that area was knee high with brushy weeds and some hardy flowers that grew in spite of the absence of care. Four O'clocks are supposed to be annuals in the northeast, but these proved Darwin's theory of survival of the fittest. Either their roots were strong enough to survive winter or they seeded themselves in the struggle to live. These little horns of sweet scent and the peppery daisies fought their way through the uncut grass for twelve years since Petros lived and died there.

Late afternoon was the lull before the storm of supper. The ladies would bustle around the kitchen and out the screen door to the large expanse of field between the house and barn. Carrie and mom were usually the first to turn those two rusty metal chairs that faced the barn in the morning to face the corner of the farmhouse that had an unobstructed view of the road and the mountain range. Aunt Helen and Aunt Christine would grab the green and white webbed folding lawn chairs that were leaning against the pump and place them in a semi circle with their seated friends. They sat like expectant theatergoers not knowing what drama would be performed. Aunt Chris would have her iced tea, while Carrie, mom and Helen held beer cans. Only Helen would pour her can of Rheingold into a glass. Slumped in a comfortable position, the ladies sat, quietly and calmly, and soaked up the last of the sunshine, knowing that children were clean from an afternoon of swimming or "creeking", and that the ordeal of supper was at least an hour or so away.

Four o'clock was the time that each little sub-group settled into a quiet hour that did not demand the constant attention of an adult. From their vantage point, the mothers could see two sides of the house where everyone under eight was within shouting distance. Michael and Gary would be squatting by the hand pump concocting mixtures of ripe berries, mud, and tree leaves. Barbara and Kathy would be playing Ginny dolls, creating houses and furniture out of sticks and stones. Jane and Elaine would be playing together as sisters or, if fighting like sisters, would split up and join the pump gang or the doll mothers. Kenny and Kenny and Jimmy and I would take advantage of being out of sight of the mothers and free from the nuisance of the little ones. The living room and porch was our private domain to listen to records, the radio or just hang out.

We all stood sentry, knowing our posts, before the frenzied feeding of the gang. Time, lulling like the setting sun, was softly muffled and we, like a cigarette after a good meal, marked the end of another adventure and settled into the unspoken, common knowledge that another day was about to wind down.

Since the farmhouse faced the road on three sides, we could all watch for the people on Hasbrouck Road coming home from work after five. Gary and Michael would wave to the man in the orange Jeep and then run to the mothers asking, "What's for dinner? We're hungry."

The lull of four o'clock became the chaos of five o'clock as the mothers deserted their lawn chairs and choreographed a supper for fourteen.

Dinnertime

The food was purchased communally from "the kitty." I don't think there was any real budget. The ladies would just throw in equal amounts of money, and, if there wasn't enough to go shopping, they would throw in more. If they had no more money, we ate spaghetti. We ate spaghetti a lot. One time we had a food fight on the porch. Strands of Ronzoni clung to the clapboard siding. I think it started with one of us remembering that Aunt Carrie said you could tell if pasta was done if it stuck to the wall. Ours was a science experiment that got out of hand. Mom stumbled upon our spaghetti sling and called the other mothers to witness our transgression. They tried to poker face their glee and made us clean the porch and then ourselves.

Everything would be washed down with Kool-Aid, which was sometimes called "Bug Juice." It came in green, yellow and shades of pinkish red. Somehow the flavor did not vary in proportion to the rainbow. We all learned the recipe: one packet, one cup sugar and fill with water to the top of the pitcher, which, thinking back, looked suspiciously like the ones at the Brauhaus Restaurant where we would eat on special occasions.

The kids ate first. There were a slew of us, so a picnic table on the front porch was where we ate. If it rained, we ate inside in the dining room. The dining room was narrow, so the huge table hugged one wall to allow a passageway along the windows from the kitchen to the front porch, and to the stairs and the living room.

Unaware of the magic that produced our supper, I imagine the ladies all took a part in preparing the meal. It was a big kitchen with a double porcelain sink that stood close to the kitchen door and under the kitchen window that faced the barn. It was the lookout window because it had a clear view of the field and the entrance to the barn. Whoever had food prep or dish duty also served as the sentry. That mom would also supervise any child labor they could Tom-Sawyer us into doing. Corn husking, bean snapping, and potato peeling were KP duties for almost-teenagers, but they didn't trust us to hull strawberries or any other treat that would taste good. Pinkerton-style moms guarded any rare and precious dessert from gangs of sweet-toothed bandits. One of them was always hovering around the fridge.

The kitchen window also faced the road as the road came from the highway to town. Anyone who drove up or by could be detected from the window. Not many cars went by. Some man in a jeep, the old-fashioned Army type, drove by at least twice a day, so he must have lived up the road and gone to work. The other neighbors had farms with chickens and hay, so they probably only drove to town once in a while. The farmhouse vacationers, with their daily forays to replenish food for fourteen people, their daily trips to the swimming hole, their trips into town for ice cream and an occasional movie, probably produced more traffic than Hasbrouck Road had ever seen. And then there were visitors. The farmhouse was a destination for day trips from Brooklyn and Astoria, Queens. They often came, those Greeks bearing gifts, with boxes of store-bought pastries that never made their way down to us kids.

The women probably ate after us and then cleaned up when we again, "went out to play." There was a TV, but it barely pulled in a visible picture with its rabbit ears. Tin foil hung off its ends like a modern mobile. No cable or satellites back then. It was almost impossible to discern figures, so we used our imagination to correspond with the sound portion. Less a television and more a radio, we still would surround it hoping to catch glimpses of a real picture if the weather would blow us some reception. When it got dark, the big dining room table became the place for cards, games, and stories. Our favorite stories were the ghost stories. Somehow, when it grew dark and the walls magnified each sound and creak, we kids became less adventuresome and independent and more secure in the pack along with our adults.

There were places that we would not go at night. No one liked being upstairs alone. When we went up the stairs, we went at the same time as the young ones, and we didn't complain. We could read or talk while the little ones dozed off. There was comfort and safety in numbers.

Some places, if there was the combined courage of two or three, might be explored cautiously during the day, but there were spots our imagination had declared off limits. Don't go down into the dirt-floored cellar, and never climb the stairs next to Aunt Carrie's room. Once we, the four oldest, did venture forth to the attic, each on a step behind each other. When Jimmy, the bravest, got to the top step to peek into the warehouse of deserted furniture and boxes, he quickly turned to run down to safety. We of the more timid nature and lower steps nearly knocked each other over following him down to the light of day and the safety of the clan. We decided to explore the attic on another day.

Four O'clock, 1943

Marika awoke to the single bong of the living room wall clock. Dozing in the chair by window, she panicked. "Is it two-thirty or three-thirty?" She didn't remember falling asleep, but the book on the carpet was testimony to the fact that she did.

Running to the clock, she could see that it was 3:33. She must have slept for two hours. The girls would be home from school soon. It only took them ten minutes to walk home from the schoolyard.

She put out Saltine Crackers with the blackberry jam her mom had made. She looked forward to the time before supper when Ann and Eleni, Marika always called Helen by her Greek name, would come bounding in with tales of classmates and school gossip. The girls fit in so well. Although they spoke Greek at home, they could speak English like an American. "The difference," Marika reassured herself, "was that they heard English all around them." She, as an immigrant girl of ten, struggled to learn a new language, and even when she did, she could not lose that Greek accent.

Demi had insisted that dinner be served at five-thirty sharp. That way he could eat and still make meetings at seven. "If I am not here, you are to eat with the girls. I want them to have a good dinner, do their homework and be in bed by eight." Sometimes Demi would not be home by eight, but he prided himself on doing the right thing as a father. Marika was not just his wife, but his nanny, cook, and governess. If he came home after eight, he would expect his supper to be warm and waiting. Marika would sit across from him and listen to all of the business Demi had accomplished that day. Eager to share his successes, even if they were always told in the future tense, Demi would mention names she did not know who would help him get his invention to the market. As he removed his cloth napkin from his lap, wiped his moustache and lips, and threw it into his plate, he would lean back in his chair, thrust out his abdomen and demand, "Tell me about Ann and Eleni's day."

After his dinner, sometimes his second one if he had come from a dinner meeting, Demi would go to the girls' bedroom, tiptoe to the bed they shared and kiss them on their foreheads.

Marika would have the dishes cleared by the time he came back to the kitchen.

"How about my day?" she said silently to herself. Thinking back through her day, she could remember nothing worth telling.

The Storm

One day, there was real danger. We had just gotten back from the swimming hole in Tillson. It was late afternoon, and we kids were hanging out on the screened porch waiting for dinner. The moms were setting the table and preparing supper.

The air became still and the sky turned a mustard-gray, casting the same sickly pallor on the mountain ridges. Then we noticed the leaves turning up to reveal their lighter undersides. As if in slow motion, we saw dark sheets of rain advancing toward us. As papers blew around the porch, we ran inside seeking shelter and shutting the door behind us.

It rumbled, thundered, and the sky emptied its bladder in torrents of rain. We watched shards of lightening, mesmerized by the free fireworks framed by the two side-by-side dining room windows.

"Get away from the windows. Close them all the way down. It's raining in."

"Aw, come-on," said Kenny G.

"No, I mean it. Go into the living room by the couch or stay here by the table. Just get away from the windows," Carrie bellowed.

When Carrie spoke, we jumped. We might have talked back to our own biological mother, but always listened to the other mothers.

We did as we were told. From the seats around the banquet table, we watched the mothers… running from place to place, shutting windows and securing doors.

They did a good job in keeping the rain from coming in through the windows, but no one could stop the rain from leaking, then pouring into the ceiling from the ancient roof.

The image of the center stairway turning into a waterfall is one that will stay with me forever. Watching Mom and Carrie sloshing up the cascading water to see what caused this flood was an image of the kind of "mother bear" courage as they directed Helen and Chris to watch the kids.

We older ones: Jimmy, Kenny G, my brother Kenny, and I had our adrenalin pumped for this exciting adventure, but the toddlers, Michael and Gary, the little ones: Jane, Elaine, whimpered as the chaos unfolded. The middle ones, Kathy and Barbara, just played little mothers protecting their "Ginny dolls." Used to spreading out in the rambling farmhouse, we looked like a refugee camp all corralled in one room. The storm continued past bedtime for all of us, so we all camped out in the living room. We were like frightened kittens that huddled closer to the mothers. By the way, it didn't really matter which mother. They were almost interchangeable in their relations to us. They were the providers and the protectors. Perhaps that's why they never told us about the farmhouse and the murder in the barn.

The next morning the sun rose, windows were opened and floors mopped. Rugs were dragged outside, buckets were emptied, and towels and bedding were spread on the line and on the grass between the house and the barn. Soggy sleeping bags from the boys' room were scattered on the lawn to dry and let that "wet boy smell" dissipate in the bright sun that followed the rain.

A trip was made with bags full of heavy sheets and blankets to the Laundromat that morning. There was a drop off service, so we knew that there would be an extra trip to town that day to pick up the cleaned and folded laundry. We were always up for another trip to town. Town was the repository of ice cream, candy and comics. The mothers would always spring for those ten cent comics like *Archie, Superman,* and *Donald Duck* because they were an investment that would pay off in some "alone time" as we kids, of all ages, passed the new comic books around and reread the old ones. Too bad we didn't save them or Jimmy's baseball cards for posterity. We could be E-Bay millionaires now.

By afternoon we were back into the routine of going to the swimming hole in Tillson. The ladies were tired and cranky and took turns sleeping on the blankets by the shore of the river. We kids only remembered the fun and excitement.

In this extended family, we learned the life-lessons of community. In adversity, our four families became one. When tragedy struck, as it did for Philanthe, family becomes the balm to soothe the hurt.

Homeo- " Pathetic" Medicine

With four mothers to attend to our safety and health, our care was a combination of basic medicine-cabinet pills and salves and Greek/Norwegian voodoo magic. In the four summers we spent at the farm, no one ever had to see a dentist or doctor. Without white uniforms or training, the mothers soothed, mended and healed all the summer accidents and ailments.

There was a drug store in the village of New Paltz, but the health and beauty aisle of the Grand Union Supermarket supplied most of our pharmaceutical needs. Aspirin was dispensed for fever or headache. Calamine Lotion was the cure for poison ivy, poison oak, sunburn or insect bites. Band-aids were dispensed with Mercurochrome that would color the wound or scrape a sickly yellowish red. Sewing needles burned with a match and then stuck through paper to sterilize them were the means to dig out splinters. For major skin problems, there was always the sanitary napkin doing double duty as a thick bandage. Who knew the many ways a feminine pad could be used? One time Aunt Christine developed a boil under her arm. I remember her wearing sleeveless blouses, ironed of course, with a Kotex sticking out covering her armpit. The drawing salve was boric acid ointment or a wet sliver of ivory soap.

When my little sister Kathy and Barbara made a tree fort out of branches and vines, my seven-year old sister came down with poison ivy. Mom cut one sanitary napkin into six little swabs and poured the calamine lotion into a bowl. The afternoon's project was to allow cousins Barbara and Jane to paint Kathy with the pink lotion. My sister held two of the cottony pieces over her eyes, leaving two circles untouched.

Usually sunburn was not a problem with so many Olive skinned Greeks, but the Norwegians were susceptible to burning. Aunt Chris always wore a sun hat, but Kenny Gundersen was fair and not about to cover his curly blond hair with a cap that was unfashionable back then. When he suffered with the sun's burning rays, the good-old sanitary napkin was dipped in cool water and olive oil and used to swab his sunburn.

Of course, those sanitary napkins were also used for their advertised purpose. With five females living so closely, the "red tent" phenomenon had us all going through "that time of month," for one would not dare speak the "P" word or use the formal "M" word. I still am amazed how "period" and "menstruating" are words used so freely by the media when we, of my generation, danced around words of a bodily or sexual nature. The jargon of the matriarchal farmhouse was developed to protect us all from the real words and the questions they might inspire. So a penis became "a thing" or a "Dupa." A vagina was identified geographically as "Down Below." Urinate was "pee pee" or "to go." Aunt Chris obfuscated it further by translating it into Norwegian. "To Go Pa Du" was a phrase understood by Greeks and Norwegians alike. A sanitary napkin was called by its brand name of Kotex. It was worn pinned to underpants or worn like a soft brick on an elastic belt that might have been the forerunner of the modern thong. During this mystical time of the month, women became sacred. No swimming and no lifting of heavy water pails. It also became the hush-hush secret to keep from Jimmy and the Kennys. God forbid males should know about females.

Chores

With fourteen people, the farmhouse operated like a camp with division of labor as its work model. There was cooking, cleaning, shopping, laundry, and constant child-minding. My mom and Aunt Carrie were the only ladies who had cars at the farm, so they were the ones to venture forth on the shopping and fetching errands. Mom had a station wagon and Aunt Carrie had a Nash Rambler, which may have been the precursor of the modern SUV.

Aunt Carrie and Jimmy and Kenny Gundersen were on a spring-water run. Aunt Carrie managed to harness "boy energy" in tasks that were both useful and fun. She would drive up the mountain road, and park just past the hairpin turn where a pipe came out of a rock of the sheer cliff that people call the "gunks." The pipe flowed all summer long with the coolest and clearest water. The pipe was only about a foot high, so lots of little containers were filled and brought back to the house for drinking. Mason jars, thermos jars, and open pails filled the back of her Nash Rambler and sloshed their way down the mountain to the kitchen. The water run was a "take me—please take me" task because Aunt Carrie didn't care how much water got splashed on the boys as long as they filled the containers.

Mom was usually the one to go grocery shopping at the Grand Union that was about six miles away in the town of New Paltz. On this particular Monday, for that was shopping day, mom took my brother Kenny and me into town. My sister Kathy was too big to fit into the child seat of the grocery cart and too little to stay "in tow" as mom filled the cart with predictable staples. She left my sister Kathy playing with her cousin Barbara, and Carrie left her Michael to play with Gary. Aunt Christine and Aunt Helen were often left as the babysitters since they did not have cars and had the youngest children. Today they planned to walk down the road to Mrs. Nachmann, the egg lady to replenish our supply. Besides, the little ones loved the adventure of hiking and picking up eggs from the hen house. Sometimes they watched how eggs were washed and candled to see which ones were fertile or not. Chris and Helen had their hands full with six little ones, so often Mrs. Nachmann would deliver eggs to the farmhouse. Somehow the eggs carried home in a basket were the most delicious though.

Vegetables were picked up at the farm stand. Since it was summer, we feasted on corn, tomatoes, peaches, cherries and plums. We would overdose on whatever was in season. We picked our own wild strawberries, black raspberries and blueberries from the field across from the farmhouse. The farmhouse land abutted the commercial orchard, and we older kids were told not to steal, but we could "gather" the ripe fruit that fell to the ground. Of course, we also picked what we could reach from the trees.

Mom would shop with the "kitty" which held the cash each family contributed, so there was a limited budget to be spent feeding ten hungry children and the four ladies. I can remember her transferring the bills from the coffee can to her purse. The only meats the ladies bought were chopped meat, chicken, and hotdogs. If there were steaks in the basket, we knew that the fathers were expected that weekend. The largest boxes of Puffed Rice, Cheerios and Kellogg's Corn Flakes were the choices for breakfast. Occasionally, there would be a banana to slice up or berries to sprinkle on the cereal, but mostly the cereal swam in a bowl of milk that we drank as a sweet treat once the cereal was gone. Spaghetti, potatoes and rice were the carbohydrates along with good old Wonder Bread with its colorful circles on the wrapper and the soft, squishy bread shaped like an oversized-cupcake. Peanut butter, grape jelly and store brand bologna were the ingredients for our lunches made with the pliable bread we preferred.

I remember that we once spread our two slices of soft bread with peanut butter and jelly and then compressed the sandwich into sticky dough that we rolled into a ball the size of a large marble. Kenny Gundersen came up with this inventive sandwich pill, and we all followed his lead giggling and screeching as we threw our sandwich balls up in the air and tried to catch them in our mouths. The mothers came in from the kitchen where the four of them had sat peacefully eating their fresh tomato with lettuce and mayo sandwiches to see why we were all so happy. I expected them to yell at us for playing with our food, but they were okay with it. In fact, I think they were secretly happy that there were no crusts or uneaten sandwiches left on the paper plates. Now, as an adult, I am amazed that we didn't get sick rolling doughy sandwiches with unwashed hands on the communal plastic tablecloth and picking up missiles from the floor to try, once again, to reach our mouths in the next throw.

On this particular trip to the supermarket, I felt special and grown up enough to speak to my mom as if she were a real person.

"Who is Philanthe?"

"Why, Carrie's mother. She is Jimmy and Michael's grandmother. She is also my aunt because she is your grandfather's sister."

Squinting and trying to connect the dots of family relatives, I pushed on, "But she seems strange. I asked her if I had any other cousins here or in Greece; she said, "Just Libby's daughter Patty. No more. Not any more. Not any more." Then she walked away and took out worry beads. Why do you all act differently when she is around?"

"Because she did have a daughter named Marika who was murdered."

"Oh, my God." I said with eyebrows pulling my eyes wide open. "How awful."

"No one talks about it so I don't know exactly what happened, but Philanthe's son-in-law went crazy and killed his family. He came up here and murdered my uncle Petros."

Mom had pulled into a parking space and turned off the ignition. It was the exclamation point to the conversation that said, "That's all I can tell you. Carrie won't talk about it and Philanthe never mentions it. Now don't you dare ask her anything about Marika. It happened a long time ago. Promise?"

I promised, but it didn't keep me from talking to Jimmy about it. After all, this was his grandmother. I bet he knew something.

Jimmy knew very little. His grandfather had died way before he was born. His grandmother never seemed strange to him because she was his grandmother, his *YiYia*. All Greek grandmothers wore black dresses and looked old fashioned. Our grandparents seemed more than a generation away from the more modern mothers. After all, our grandparents came from a country foreign and strange to our American ways. We grandkids never held conversations with the old Greeks. We allowed them to pinch us, hug us, give us treats like Chiclets and dollar bills, but there was never really communication. Hell, we rarely talked to our parents except to ask and answer questions of immediacy.

"My mom sometimes talks about her sisters, and I know she only has one sister. Libby is her older sister. I think she had another, but I don't know what happened to her."

"Could she have been murdered?"

"I can't imagine that she was murdered, but no one ever talks about her."

" Maybe she just died." I offered as an explanation to my own questions. "I know my mom had sisters, twins, who died when they were babies. There was a worldwide flu in 1917 that killed lots of people. My mom also had an older sister named Poppi. I have seen pictures of her. I think she died as a teenager. I think she had bone cancer. They say she looked a lot like me. They say she was pretty."

At the word "pretty," Jimmy playfully punched to top of my arm. I didn't know if he wanted to move from the uncomfortable topic, or if he just reacted to my self-compliment. "Yeah, pretty. Was she conceited like you too?"

The next time the murders came up as a topic of conversation, Jimmy and I made up our own version of the murders. We decided that the madman escaped from a mental institution, came up here and kidnapped his family and tied them to the old scary tree across the street. We couldn't bring ourselves to add details beyond that. We scared ourselves in knowing that we could have been connected to a murder. The fact that the victims were faceless names, even though they were relatives, helped us to be indifferent to the tragedy. I think if we had known the extent of the horror, we would not have been able to enjoy those carefree summers.

I believe that the Greeks just don't speak of sadness; they just bury it along with bad memories. Philanthe had come back to the farm that summer of 1956 because her family was there. Family was a stronger tie than fear, or revenge. In the card game of life, joy trumped sadness any day of the week.

Philanthe's visit to the farm in New Paltz

While the four families vacationed in the farmhouse, we would often have the "Older Greeks" visit, mostly on a Sunday. Mostly it was Uncle Pete, not to be confused with his brother Petros, and Philanthe. Uncle Gregory and Aunt Georgia sometimes drove up to the country for the day. Those were the only Greeks I knew, and I was not sure how they were all related to me or to each other. Now I know that there were at least ten siblings, some who stayed in Greece or returned to Greece. I have a feeling there were more who died young or at birth.

Philanthe was Carrie's mother. That made her Jimmy and Michael's grandmother or *YiYia*. I don't think we thought beyond that. We just never analyzed the family tree when we were so busy swinging on the branches. Philanthe would have been my great aunt because she was my grandfather's, Aristomenes, little sister.

Philanthe looked old, but, in fact, she was younger than I am now. She was in her sixties, and, since she was a widow, she wore her black "*YiYia*" dress. It was cotton, short sleeved, below-the-knee length, with buttons up the front. It was the old lady dress that all Greeks, at a certain age, wore as a uniform that said, "I'm done. I am not looking to date. I have had my family. Let me now be the grandmother. It's your turn to live." The dress was completed with black orthopedic shoes. They usually had short, sturdy, blocks for heels, and were worn with cotton stockings. Philanthe sometimes wore little white cotton anklets on top of the stockings. Most old Greek ladies had bunions (don't know why), so their shoes, which were worn every day, took on the shape of the crooked toes. I imagine all the crones and hags of fairytales and mythology were modeled on the Greek *YiYia*.

I only remember Philanthe visiting the farm twice. I know she never stayed over. She would just visit for the day and return with whatever relative brought her up to the country. She may have been there more often, but we paid little attention to visitors. We almost-teenagers would politely accept hugs and greetings and then voluntarily make ourselves scarce so the grown ups could visit. Philanthe had long gray hair that was pulled straight back from her face in a very thin bun worn high on the back of her head. Her face was small and the features were all nice, but together she looked like a feminine version of my Uncle Gregory. What I remember most about her was her belly. She was tiny in stature, but she had a bloated belly that made her look silly. She looked like a seventy-year old pregnant lady. Perhaps her bulging belly made her self-conscious because she always crossed her arms across her abdomen as if she were trying to hide it. Over-compensating for the belly protrusion, she appeared to be leaning backward to balance her weight so her blue eyes looked skyward instead of straight ahead.

Philanthe didn't say much, at least to us kids. She did the typical Greek greeting. We braced ourselves for the hug and double kiss and the claiming of kin. "You look just like your mother. You two could be sisters." Then as an aside, to the grown-ups, because Greeks always protect their young from misfortune, "She is the spitting image of Poppi. Tch, Tch." The tongue sucking punctuated the fact that something sad had been resurrected from the past.

I probably knew that Poppi was mom and Helen's older sister. She had died at sixteen of some bone infection or cancer. Again, we were only spoon fed unhappiness. I think they, the adults, thought our weak stomachs, minds and hearts could not comprehend or accept the darker side of life. I had seen pictures of Poppi, and, yes, there was that DNA producing in me a mirror version a generation later.

Philanthe visited with the adults, but she seemed intrigued by the games and solitaire that we older kids were playing on the porch under the buggy lights. She spoke to me as I was about to deal out another hand of solitaire. As I turned up the initial seven face cards, she would viscerally react to each number and suit. "Cards tell stories," she said, and she said she would tell my fortune with the cards. She taught me the meanings of the good and bad suits and the special cards, like the nine of clubs that meant a letter was coming. Over time she taught me how to tell fortunes using regular playing cards.

Not only cards told stories; dreams did also. "Oh, teeth mean death. Brush your teeth as bedtime, so the ritual of doing so won't prey on your mind. Never dream of teeth." Then she chuckled, "As if we could control our dreams. They are only messages."

She also objected to certain combinations of food. One time she nearly spilled the glass of milk as she snatched it to replace it with water or juice. She warned me about eating grapes and drinking milk. "Grapes are good, but not with milk."

There were no small talks, no sharing of opinions, no anecdotes, and no questions from Philanthe. She hovered and kibitzed and gave answers to unasked questions. She gave small hints for living. "Don't eat this, don't fight, and always love your family." Always, she left pinching your cheek saying, "Be a good girl. Be safe and be good to your parents." Philanthe delivered sermons in cards, in dreams, in food, and in etiquette.

What did we know of Philanthe? She was Jimmy and Michael's grandmother, his *YiYia*; she was Aunt Carrie's mother.

What we didn't know is that Philanthe was a survivor. She knew to put tragedy behind her and face the next day when the sun would surely rise once again with no regard for the sorrow of yesterday.

Evening Walk

At dusk, the day's colors of the road and fields around the farmhouse melted together in the hot July night blending the landscape into indistinct shapes and shadows. Our world divided itself into two domains, the inside and the outside. The property outside looked like an old black and white photograph faded into shades of all gray.

The grown-ups were sitting out on the screened porch with the bare yellow bulb casting a slash of yellow turning the red checked oilcloth orange at the center of the picnic table. There were remnants of the adult dinner: ash trays held some cigarettes smoked to a centimeter of the white filter with some longer unfiltered ones that look oval rather than round; coffee cups are sipped to their coffee ground sludge, and a bakery box still holds the last Danish that has been abandoned for the sake of etiquette.

The little ones: Jane, Elaine, Gary and Michael, were already put to bed. The younger ones, Kathy and Barbara, were building houses with the domino set on the dining room table. The company had just left, and the four ladies were luxuriating in the quiet moment of freedom—freedom from the little ones and freedom from playing hostesses to Pete and Eva who drove up from Bayside for an afternoon visit.

We older kids, Jimmy, Kenny Gundersen and I, said we were going to take a walk. There was never traffic on the road that wound around the farmhouse at a right angle. Kenny, although three years younger, insisted that he be allowed to go with us.

"Oh, take him with you." Mom insisted.

"But we're going to walk all the way to Nachmann's, and it'll be dark on the way back."

"Take flashlights," Carrie suggested. We had already thought of that. We may have been older, but what was familiar during the day became frightening at night, especially the tree. We had heard that there was a terrible murder there. There was a big open field that tumbled down a hill to the valley below, and, if you looked out, all you could see were the rocky cliffs of the Shawangunks. The scary tree stood alone in a silhouette against the pastoral scenery. It was twisted and gnarled and lacked leaves on one side. It was dark against the sky because the sun had slid behind the cliffs on that side of the mountain. At night, the tree stretched out its limbs like a boogie man ready to grab children who ventured too close to its home on the side of the road directly in front of the farmhouse. We always felt safer when we passed the tree and were out of sight of the farmhouse and the grown-ups. After a few twists and turns of the dirt road, we could see the light of the Nachmann house up the road. We walked slower.

I had scrounged two long cigarette butts and had kitchen matches in my pocket. My big score was the whole oval Turkish cigarette from the pack that Pete and Eva had brought up for Carrie and Min. Aunt Carrie stuck her pack of Kools inside her shorts' pocket, but mom would always leave hers on the dining room table. Pete was Carrie's younger brother, and Eva was his wife. They were supposed to bring Philanthe, Carrie and Peter's mother, up for the day, but at the last minute Philanthe decided to stay home.

Midway, out of sight of the aunts, I would light up and offer drags to my cousins Jimmy and Kenny. Jimmy didn't really smoke, but he would join me in a puff or two. My cousin Kenny would also take a drag and choke and cough. He wasn't about to be called a sissy. My little brother Kenny who tagged along was sworn to secrecy. He never told, but I felt blackmailed by him when he would give me that "I can tell" look when he didn't get his way. I think it was hard for him to be the only boy between the younger girls and us older kids who were all twelve—almost grown-up. After all, I had my period. Jimmy had hair under his arms, and Kenny... well, Kenny still looked younger even though we three cousins had been born within three months of each other in 1944.

One of the purposes of our night walk was to get away from the aunts, to have a smoke, and to discuss those "girl-boy" topics. We told dirty jokes that we didn't quite get and shared our friends' romantic and sexual exploits. We played an unannounced game of "one-upmanship" as we told about anonymous scandals that may or may not have been true. We compiled our adolescent discoveries with a safe and platonic synergy. We liked being out from under the eyes of all the aunts, especially today with the company from the city.

Pete and Eva had only come up for the day. They brought the ladies bakery treats, cigarettes, and a watermelon for us kids. They left right after the adult dinner, and they couldn't understand how the aunts would let us older cousins walk down the road at night.

"Who were they again?" Kenny Gundersen asked as we passed the brook.

"Peter is my uncle," Jimmy explained. "He is my mother's younger brother."

"So he is Aunt Carrie's brother?" I restated as if I finally figured out which old Greek belonged to which other Greek.

"Right, they have the same mother. My *YiYia* is Philanthe." Jimmy knew who Philanthe was, but Kenny G, Kenny and I had no clue. Jimmy couldn't see our blank faces, but he filled the confused silence with more information. "Your grandfather and my grandmother are sister and brother."

"Not you." Jimmy said to Kenny Gundersen. "I have no idea how you are related to us. You're not even Greek."

"I know. I'm Norwegian. I'm related to Carol because my grandmother and her grandmother were sisters. I can't figure out who belongs to who at the farmhouse. "Whom," I corrected.

"Whom what?" Kenny snapped.

"Related to whom?" I persisted.

"Whom gives a shit?" Kenny Gundersen spat at me.

"No, it's 'Who gives a shit.'" Jimmy piped in. A friendly jab to Kenny Gundersen's shoulder let him know that grammar is off topic.

"So whom was Eva?" Kenny Gundersen persisted.

"Who," I corrected.

"Cut it out, you two," Jimmy said walking between us to prevent us from continuing our grammatical warfare. "Peter is my uncle. He is two years younger than my mother."

"I get it." My little brother even figured that one out. "They're married. Can't you tell? They kept looking at each other. He kept putting his arm around her whenever they talked about that woman."

"What woman?" I asked.

"Phil-something."

"Philanthe," Jimmy said. "My grandmother. That's who we were just talking about. Philanthe is my *YiYia*."

"But we have a *YiYia* too." My little brother added confusing himself more.

"*YiYia* is Greek for grandmother, so everyone has a *YiYia*." Jimmy said as if that cleared up the relationship.

"I don't." said Kenny Gundersen, "I have a Nana."

"Well, I have a Nana too," concluded my brother Kenny.

"Shit." Jimmy said. "Who cares. We're all cousins."

"She sure was nervous, wasn't she?" Kenny Gundersen asked remembering what Eva had said when we said we were talking a walk down the road to the egg lady's house.

"It's not safe," Eva had warned.

"Of course it is," Aunt Carrie countered as she turned sideways on the picnic bench, pulled her knees up, and leaned on the table with one elbow and smoked with her other.

"Aren't they afraid?" Pete asked as he tried to extricate himself awkwardly from the cage of the bench that was attached to the oversized, homemade picnic table.

"No, Pete. They don't know. They're kids. They don't know to be afraid." Carrie whispered and glared as she swung her body the rest of the way out of the table.

She led her brother and sister-in-law into the house, through the dining room, and out through the kitchen door. Their car was parked there, and they hugged and said prolonged goodbyes.

"Yes," Peter admitted. "It's guess it's better that way. Maybe next time we can get Philanthe to visit. It might help her to see this old place swarming with kids and dogs and these damn mosquitoes," Peter said swatting his arm that was still outside the car resting on the driver's side window.

Pete and Eva drove the five miles to town before Eva spoke. "How can they stay there? In that house? I could never…"

Sundays

The best thing about a summer when you are twelve is that everyday is a duplicate of the day before in an eternal calendar of days that seemed to stretch out forever. It was hard to discern a Tuesday from a Thursday, but Sundays were different. Sundays were muffled and muted, and we viscerally knew to be a little quieter to let the mothers and fathers sleep a little longer. We were kittens scampering around the downstairs and the back lawn testing our boundaries but knowing not to stray too far from the litter. When the coffee pot burped and wheezed and filled the air with a prelude to breakfast, we would make our way back to the safe proximity of our own family. It was the one time that we ate with our adults. The four families spread out to every surface on the porch, the dining room and the kitchen.

Sunday breakfast was more than flakes shaken from a box into a sea of milk. Sunday morning promised bacon and eggs and lots of toast with jam. There was never enough bacon. To this day, bacon is always a rationed treasure that seems dearer because of its rarity. The eggs were plentiful and golden. Scrambled eggs were the color of sunshine, and eggs, over easy, looked like a Hawaiian sunset. Eggs from Mrs. Nachmann were so fresh that they couldn't be hard-boiled. The shells would cling to the egg white.

The afternoon was spent in slow motion. Whatever the activity, it was done savoring the last moments the fathers would be there. On weekends, there would usually be my dad's car, Uncle Joe's car, and Uncle Goldie's pick-up truck giving us the option of splitting up the mob to go in separate directions. At times the grassy field from the house to the barn resembled a used car lot.

The evening barbecue took on the aura of "The Last Supper" with steaks and salad for the adults and hamburger and hotdogs and chips for the kids. As dinner was put away, we watched the fathers loading up the cars to head home to work. Goldie Gundersen would drive to Staten Island to walk high steel constructing skyscrapers in Manhattan. Uncle Joe Vecchione would head home to Roosevelt, Long Island to get a short night of sleep before resuming his butter and egg route for institutions in Brooklyn. My father would return to Freeport, Long Island to operate his restaurant machinery distributorship in Nassau County. Bill Jacobs would return to Brooklyn to set type for a newspaper. The workweek was a world of testosterone leaving the estrogen-laden farm to be run like a matriarchal society for the weekdays, a duty they gratefully relinquished to the patriarchs each weekend.

Sunday night felt like a clock unwinding. We were a little more tired. We could feel the night as a heavy blanket beckoning us to resist the fight to stay up "just a little longer."

Sunday morning 1943

Marika padded into the kitchen to make coffee and a substantial breakfast for the family. She would love to have bacon or ham to go with the eggs she brought home from the farm in New Paltz. She reminded herself that she was fortunate to have the eggs. She placed two slices of bread in the toaster and took the jam, made without sugar, from the cupboard. Uncle Petros grew strawberries that were sweet enough to stew with pectin to resemble jam.

Demi entered the kitchen dressed in a shirt and tie. Her nightgown hung on her skinny frame in contrast to her well-dressed husband. He hovered in back of her as she prepared the eggs by whisking them in a bowl.

"I'll have mine over-easy," he demanded. "The girls can have them scrambled. I wouldn't want you to waste those eggs."

Marika kept scrambling with her right hand and reached for another bowl to do two eggs for her husband.

"Why do you need a bowl? Just crack them on the edge of the fry pan. Can't you do that?" He turned and took his place at the kitchen table where his coffee cup was waiting for him. Marika quickly took the percolator off the stove and poured him a cup, black, no sugar. She remembered that he once drank it with cream and sugar, Greek style with the cream warmed so it didn't cool down the coffee. Now he insisted that he preferred it black without sugar rather than admit how expensive and rare those additions were.

Marika gently cracked two eggs into the bowl and slid them into the second fry pan. "Eat your eggs, girls. They came from Uncle Petros' neighbor in New Paltz."

Ann and Helen, dressed for Sunday 11:00 o'clock service at St. Helene's Greek Orthodox Church, sat at the table and poured themselves milk from the bottle. The cream had been skimmed off and saved for a special treat with berries gathered upstate.

"Why can't I have mine fried like daddy?" Helen asked looking across at her father who was sipping his coffee.

"I've already scrambled yours. That's why. I know...I will eat yours and fry another for you. How do you want it?"

"Just like daddy's," Helen answered catching her father's smile as she said it.

Marika watched her family eat quickly, leave their plates and excuse themselves to get ready to walk to church.

"Why aren't you coming, mother?" asked Ann knowing that her mom had missed many Sundays because she was "away again" to quiet her nerves. This time she had not gone to "that hospital," but Marika and the girls had spent a week upstate with her YiYia Philanthe and Uncle Petros.

"I'll go next time," Marika offered as she sat down at the table to eat her cold scrambled eggs.

Demi ushered the girls ahead of him and followed them down the steps. He grabbed each by the hand as they crossed the busy boulevard for the three-block walk to church. Demi was glad Marika was not going. He would show his darling girls to his neighbors without having to include Marika in the conversations. He would just say, "She is away again."

Last Day of Summer

"I can't sleep with that racket," my sister complained that last Saturday night at the farm. "Why can't I stay up? It's the last night."

"Those are the katydids, Kathy."

"The what?"

"Katydids. They're like crickets. Supposedly they are speaking to one another. One says, 'Katy did' and the other answers 'Katy didn't.'"

"Didn't what?"

"Didn't keep pestering," my mom said sweetly as she lifted my little sister from the double bed they shared. "Actually, I don't know what they are saying. I only know that we only hear them at the end of summer. Now, be quiet so you don't wake your cousins. The big kids are on the porch. One half-hour. That's all you get." It was easy to give in knowing that Kathy, who got car sick, would be sleepy from the medicine that would save the rest of us from making "Whoops" stops along the side of the road. Kathy always got to ride up front between mom and dad.

You could tell summer was ending even without the incessant calls of the katydids. It would start getting dark even before the last dish was cleared from the picnic table. We would have to grab a sweatshirt for our walk up Hasbrouck Road. We would snuggle under the scratchy wool blankets and rush to the warmth of the kitchen stove the first thing in the morning.

The fathers were up this weekend because they would load up the cars and drive us home on Sunday. We would have one week before school starts after Labor Day. When the fathers are up, we kids would get away with murder because the watchful eyes of the moms were turned away from us and toward their husbands.

We looked in the corner cupboard for the flashlights and found some candles.

"Can we take these candles with us on the walk?" We had found some punks and dried them in the sun. We wanted to light them and keep the mosquitoes away and carry them as torches up the road.

Receiving no reply, we assumed permission and bolted out the porch door with our forbidden booty. Three Olsens, one Jacobs and one Gundersen bravely walked out into the dark, half-mooned, night toward the ugly tree. Kathy, thrust into a teenage adventure at age eight, now wanted the safety of her bed. Grabbing her hand, I handed her a lit punk and said, "Just you shush up." Off we went into the darkening night.

The road ahead seemed to be swallowed up in the black night. Trees and bushes blurred the road, so we hung back in the mustard glow of the bug light on the screened porch. We moved a safe distance from the fearful tree but did not turn the bend where it was safe to light up a cigarette. With flashlights and punks glowing, a small drag on a cigarette would not be noticeable to our parents, who were in the yard just outside the kitchen door.

We could hear the grown ups laughing and their conversation was just white noise in counterpoint to the cacophony of the katydids.

We cousins didn't really talk to each other that night. We had said it all in the four weeks we spent at the farm. We now felt comfortable enough to not speak. We could just be together, in the dark, safely distant from yet connected to the farmhouse and to each other. As we huddled, the yellows and ambers of flashlights, punks and cigarettes illuminated only our faces. Hazy portraits of children looked older as we realized that tomorrow would separate us, but the bond of family could always bring us back to this time and place.

"Jeez, it's getting cold. I'm going back," Kenny G announced as he aimed his flashlight up the bend in the road. "Are you coming?"

Like a drum major, he lead the way past the ferocious tree hastening his steps as he passed the huge maple whose roots had encroached on the dirt road. We fell into cadence and sprinted the last hundred steps to where the grown-ups sat in lawn chairs around the glow of charcoal embers still smelling of steak and hamburgers.

"Get to bed kids," Carrie commanded.

Prolonging the moment with kisses and "good-nights" we filed through the kitchen screen door which seemed to scream in the night air, a sound very different from its morning swish. The yellow light above the dining room table showed us the way. Boys rounded the corner to the living room hovel. My sister and I tiptoed up the stairs to our bedroom. We used our flashlight so we didn't shine the hall light into the three other bedrooms where our five youngest cousins slept soundly.

I tucked Kathy in and then checked the closet to make sure all my stuff was packed for the trip home. On the top shelf was a letter, and under it was a small circle of gold. The note was addressed to *Theo Petros*. I deliberated. "Should I open it?" The paper was yellowed and brittle, and whatever glue may have held it together, gave way as I slid my fingers under the flap. "Thank you for our week at the farm. We had a very nice time. Love, Helen and Ann. P.S. I liked feeding the chickens-Ann." A browned, thin-skinned daisy was stuck to the note. Someone must have pressed it in a book with tissue paper.

When Kathy was purring and curled into a kitten comma, I snuck downstairs and out the kitchen door that now crooned a soft night song. "Hey, look what I found in the closet. It's a letter to Theo Petros. Who is he?"

It became so quiet that I could hear Aunt Carrie breath through her nose.

"Can I see it?" my mom asked permission in slow motion. Even the katydids abruptly ended their evening chatter.

"Sure. And I found a bracelet too. It looks like a ring of daisies. Do I have to return it?" I asked taking the bangle from my wrist, hoping for a-finders-keepers, and handing it to mom.

Mom had read the letter and passed it to Aunt Carrie who turned her back to us and read it in the light of the barbecue grill. I thought I saw a small flare of light as if brittle paper hit smoldering embers.

"No, honey. You can keep it." Aunt Carrie said without turning to face me.

"Thanks," I said as I put the bracelet back on my wrist and danced back upstairs with my treasure.

I wore the bracelet to bed and savored the moment of winning a prize. I could hear the parents talking outside the bedroom window, but the night sounds muffled their words. I could not discern the lyrics, but the melody was a sad, end of summer song.

Marika's Summer
at the Farm 1943

During the summer of 1943, the world in upstate New York seemed strangely quiet and calm considering the chaos of the war in Europe. Daily life was a mechanical series of human events. People worked; people ate; people went to school. People went on with their very common lives against a backdrop of suppressed, intense emotions of fear and confusion. The repetitious humdrum of day-to-day routine was contrapuntal to the din of battles and death. All the newspapers were filled with death tolls or accounts of victories. Pictures of servicemen were displayed as they were deployed or returning home.

Marika's younger brother Peter was overseas, in Europe she thought, but who could be sure? Letters came to her mother with phrases blackened out by the censors. When they were read aloud in their fragmented pieces, they said nothing really. "Miss you…wish I was home…I'm okay. How's Carrie? Marika, and Libby? Love you, mom." No information, just kind messages to span the miles and months. To Philanthe, his mom, it was all that needed to be said.

Demi was forty-two, too old to serve in the army. He felt cowardly safe in a storm of battle. Not draftable but feeling survivor's guilt as he went about raising a family and earning a decent living while men just a decade younger put their lives on hold and in danger. "Not my fault," he would tell himself. "Can't leave

Marika and the girls to fend for themselves." He was a civilian in a world focused on soldiers.

Summer was hot and long in the city, so Marika looked forward to spending two weeks with her mother and uncle in New Paltz. Demi was not so thrilled. Why travel hours away from home to a place lacking the very comforts he had in their apartment in Queens? For the girls, Anne and Helen, it was fun to pump the water and use the outhouse. For them it was not an inconvenience; it was an adventure and an exotic setting to weave stories to share with their girlfriends back home who were spending each day in the coolness of the park down the street from their homes.

What Demi especially did not like was being a guest of Petros, Philanthe's youngest brother. Marika's uncle was only a few years older than Demi, but Demi always felt unequal to this man who was his contemporary. Petros, like all the Takis brothers, was self-assured with the overflow of self-confidence earned by brothers who had already made their fortunes in real estate and in business. The two men, Petros and Demi, were close in age but as different as could be in their view of the world they shared. Petros was casually gracious and accommodating. Demi was introverted and exacting. While Petros saw the big picture, Demi saw only the myopic details.

One time, when Demi was trying to describe his invention that would dispense tickets for a cafeteria style restaurant, Petros heard only the word "restaurant" and began to tell about the latest restaurant, called Gregory's after one of his brothers, that Aris and Gregory had bought in Brooklyn. The invention and its ability to produce tickets got lost in the news of brothers unafraid to speculate in this post depression time. Even the process of patenting and prototyping mirrored Demi's personality. He was precise. He dressed as a man who had already reached success. His hat was creased just so and his tie never askew. His work, his attire, his family, his invention were the mirrors of his self esteem. As a mechanical engineer, his work was precise. Demi was precise and unwavering in his plans. He liked his life, his wife, and his children just so. "Controlling" would be the word Philanthe used to describe her son-in-law. Things got done "his way." He could only see things through his own eyes and could never imagine another point of view.

Conversely, Petros and the brothers were swept along in the family's whirlwind of investment and management. Petros, the only unmarried brother, had tried the restaurant business. He just didn't get caught up in it. He would tend bar and prefer to talk to the customers. Aris and Gregory and their nephews were the owners and managers who worked so they could expand or add to their holdings. Petros was content to work and get a paycheck.

When he bought the farm, Petros thought it would be a good place for the family to visit. His nephew Peter, Philanthe's youngest and only son, suffered from asthma, so Philanthe and the children would spend summers in the country. Later, when Petros tired of the demands of working weekends and nights in the restaurant business, he moved up to the Catskills and worked in a defense plant in Poughkeepsie. He was content to do the line work to earn enough to maintain the farm and his casual lifestyle. A small victory garden and a few chickens were all he wanted. He was proud of the many stores and restaurants of his siblings, but Petros preferred the quiet and simple life style of the farm. It reminded him of his home in Greece. He would walk out the kitchen door and sit on one of four metal lawn chairs that faced toward the road, the barn and the Shawangunk Mountains beyond the fields. He had the company of his co-workers and the comfort of neighbors who waved and dropped by for a courtesy call.

As a single man, Petros encouraged the family members to come visit. The farmhouse was large and the lifestyle relaxed. Philanthe and her children would come up to New Paltz as often as they could. It was a place so unpretentious that all who came to visit felt at home. Only Demi felt like an unwanted guest. Demi would accompany his family upstate on a Sunday, stay for the midday meal then travel home to get back to work. "You stay with your family," he would say to Marika. "I need to go to this meeting and see some person about something." Marika could fill in the blanks. These were men of his realm. They were names without faces. Bankers, engineers, inventors, men of business belonged in his world of work. Her contacts were grocers, dentists, and teachers. The name of Demi's important contact was just one more thing she and her husband did not share. He called Petros and her other uncles "her family." It was *his* family if the four of them could be alone. If he had relatives living in America, they were not invited to share their private lives. He did not want to share his wife and girls with others. He jealously guarded them from the Takis family. He especially disliked this young uncle, called "Theo" for uncle in Greek, who made Marika smile and laugh.

Marika and the children spent the two weeks, and when Demi came by train and then taxi to bring them home, the girls begged to stay another week. Here their mother was relaxed. She laughed. She slept late. She played cards with her mother and Theo. They swam in the river and played in the brook. They made garlands of daisies and danced in the fields pretending to be fairies and elves. They picked strawberries and wild blueberries.

Quietly, the girls gathered their belongings and followed their parents to the taxi.

"Papa, we picked berries and YiYia put them on pancakes with real whipped cream, sugared cream."

Marika added, "Imagine, sugar is such a wartime rarity, and they had it with breakfast."

"Impossible," he replied. With a single word, Demi had brought two weeks of fun to an end.

She had a sudden urge to yell, "Stop" to the taxi driver, get out, run away, hand in hand with her daughters, leaving this man who could eclipse her sun with a single look or a single word. "Impossible," she swallowed the word and closed her eyes to turn off his toxic, suffocating hold on her happiness.

Marika was barely eight when she accompanied her mother to America with her older sister Libby, who was ten. Barely the age of her youngest daughter, she would try to remember the bucolic life in the Greek village. Chickens and goats, good food, hugs, the protection of family and neighbors. The absence of her father was compensated *by the lavish love of her mother. What she could not recall in facts and history, she could relive in the warm feeling of sunshine. She could picture a little girl, herself or maybe her daughter Helen, dancing with arms outstretched and face turned to the morning sun.*

When life got too hard to face, she would retreat into these images and feelings that she would write and rewrite into stories of Greek childhood that promised her so much more than Demi was willing to give her.

On the train home, Ann and Helen gave him a running commentary about what they did each day and who they saw and what they ate.

"I fed corn to Theo's chickens, father," bragged Helen who was considered too young last summer to walk to the barn alone.

"Did you know that Mrs. Nachmann has chickens that lay colored eggs?" added Ann who was aware of the pregnant silence that intensified the lack of conversation between her parents.

"No, I didn't." their father replied.

"Easter eggs, she calls them. Some are green and some are blue."

"No kidding! Did she dye them just to fool you?"

"No, really. The chickens lay them that way."

Turning to Marika, Demi said in a hushed and snarly undertone, "Speaking of laying, what did you do these two weeks?"

Covering the deliberate double entendre, Marika answered her husband by saying, "The girls and I took walks, and swam and picked berries. It was a good vacation."

"That's nice." Demi replied with a voice that sounded warm to the girls but was coldly accompanied by a frozen stare that looked out from narrowed eyes and a furrowed brow.

It was a long and quiet ride back to Ozone Park. There were no smiles and no laughs. Soon it would be back to the routine of school.

Not-so-good Morning

September 1943

Marika loved to get up early. She would listen to the morning sounds of the street through the open windows. Vendors and merchants would attend to the daily liturgy of opening doors, cranking awnings and moving produce around. The girls would need to be woken soon, so she savored the few quiet moments as she listened to the Pyrex coffee pot wheeze and burp as a prelude to that first cup of dark, rich coffee. Her brother had given her a few tins of this real coffee that he had gotten with ration cards, not that chicory substitute, before he left to go into the Army. She normally would mix it with the ersatz "coffee" to stretch it out. This morning it was real coffee through and through, and the smell of it overpowered last night's braised lamb shank. It wafted memories of years ago when there was no war, when the girls were young, and when Demi kissed her "Good Morning." Years ago life was better when there was real coffee.

Marika ushered Annie and Helen through the morning routine trying to quell the high-pitched voices of her girls who were eager to meet their friends and walk to school. "Don't wake your father, Annie," Marika warned. "He went out after supper and came home late last night. He's meeting with those men about that invention." Annie was in eighth grade and more interested in her girl and boy friends than in the academics of civics and grammar.

Besides, it came so easy to her that she didn't have to exert much effort to get A's and B's. Helen, on the other hand, was the student who did more than asked to please her teacher. She worked her hardest and earned B's and C's. Marika was proud of her daughters. They fit in so nicely with their classmates. She remembered when she came to America, at Helen's age actually, and struggled to learn the American ways and the language that never followed the grammar rules she memorized.

With the girls out the door with books and lunch in hand, Marika sat down once again in the easy chair by the window that faced the street. Coffee cup in hand, unsweetened with the scarcity of sugar these days, she put her feet up on the coffee table and let her head fall back on the plump pillow. She was still wearing mule slippers, a cotton nightgown and a chenille robe to neutralize the cooler nights of late September. She should get up and get dressed, but it was so comfortable to just sit here sipping real coffee and knowing that she would have the whole day to herself as soon as Demi left for work. He had said that he needed to meet with those men again to discuss the patent and would not be home for dinner. Maybe she and the girls would get root-beer floats at the candy store down at the corner.

Demi came out of the bedroom completely dressed including his hat that he carried in his left hand. He always carried it by the crown making sure that the crease was perfectly formed and the brim untouched.

"Good Morning," Marika said as he passed by her on the way to the kitchen.

He emerged with a coffee cup in his right hand, taking sips as he walked around the living room collecting a folder of papers, his briefcase, and the hat that he had momentarily placed on the end table on the far side of the room.

"Good Morning, I said," repeated Marika.

He looked at her, mumbled, and continued to gather the things he would need for the day at the plant and the meeting with his partners.

"I said, 'Good Morning,'" Marika attempted once more.

"See you tonight," Demi said as he walked away from her and out the door. "Don't have the girls wait for supper. I have a dinner engagement with potential backers," he added from the stoop side of the door as he pulled the door toward himself with a vengeance. It was the exclamation point to his exit.

As the silence followed the slam of the front door, Marika sat holding her cup midway between the coffee table and her lips. When she sipped it, it was cold. She walked to the kitchen sink and watched the brown stain on the white porcelain as she poured out the remaining mouthful of coffee.

Easter Vacation 1944

Marika and the girls were savoring their final days of Easter vacation with Theo Petros and YiYia Philanthe. On Sunday Petros said he would drive them back to the city. Marika would be home in time to make Demi his dinner and get the girls ready for school on Monday.

Today, Friday, they were going to dye eggs in the red food coloring so YiYia could bake them into the braided bread for Easter breakfast. Even though it was the Christian Good Friday, Petros had to report to work to complete a government contract. It bothered him little since this holiday was the American Easter. He still celebrated Greek Easter according to the Greek calendar. His grandnieces were happy to celebrate both dates by adapting the Greek traditions to the customs of hiding eggs and perhaps finding a precious piece of chocolate on Sunday morning.

Marika and the girls had spent the morning baking koulouria, *anisette biscuits made from the precious sugar and flour they had saved for this special occasion. They had used up all the eggs they had gathered from the barn. In better times, the family would have roasted a young lamb, but no lamb was to be had. Philanthe would make* kiftithes *instead. The dried mint for the meatballs, made with more bread than meat, had come from Petros' victory garden.*

"We will need some more eggs to dye for the egg fights," Ann announced at lunchtime. Traditionally, each guest would get a red

egg, symbolic of the blood of Christ, to challenge all others. One by one, a person would hold his egg out to be hit by another egg. Whosever egg survived the thumping would go on to challenge another. Techniques were practiced. Some thought that you could hold your egg round side up to defensively absorb the shock; others thought that the pointed end was stronger and should be used offensively. Pride in eating a winning, un-cracked hardboiled egg could be seen in the smile of the victor.

"We'll walk up to Mrs. Nachmann's to get more eggs, but first I want you girls to write a nice thank-you note to Theo *for the wonderful week we spent here on the farm."*

Marika, and her daughters wrote a short note and added a pressed daisy to the plain note- paper. It was actually Helen's idea to add the daisy since her uncle had given Marika a bracelet he found at work. Petros had tried to find its owner, but no one at the Poughkeepsie defense plant had claimed it. The daisies reminded him of the flowers they would pick in the summer. Philanthe, meanwhile, placed the still-warm Greek cookies on a small white plate and covered them with wax paper.

"I am ready when you are, Marika," she called from the kitchen. "We'll bring Mrs. Nachmann some cookies," Philanthe added when she recalled a familiar phrase from her childhood. "Never return an empty dish." In the country, Mrs. Nachmann was the closest person to a friend.

The three generations strolled down the country road wearing only sweaters on this fine spring day. They had just turned up the steep driveway to the "egg lady's" house, and they could hear the chickens clucking and chatting in the yard. The hens scattered when they heard what sounded like gunshots. They ran to the front door as Mrs. Nachmann opened it in anticipation. She too had heard the shots followed by glass shattering.

"It sounds like a car back-firing down the road," her husband explained as he joined the ladies at the doorstep. Come on in."

Just then more shots echoed off the mountains. "Too many shots to be a car backfiring," Mr. Nachmann said as he turned an ear up the road and furrowed his brows. "Is Petros home?"

"No." Marika quickly added, "He's at the plant, and we're all here."

"I'll drive up to see. You stay here with the Missus."

As he rounded the turn past the Takis farmhouse in his 1940 Ford truck, he passed a man dressed as if he were going to a funeral. He was wearing an overcoat and dress hat even though he was overdressed for both the weather and the location. The man came around the farmhouse and continued to shoot out the windows. One by one, he was aiming and firing at every window in the place. Mr. Nachmann turned the truck around in the driveway and retraced the road to where the stranger was turned with gun aimed at the second floor bedroom windows.

He drove past the man and came to a stop about fifty feet ahead of the shooter. Careful to push out only the driver's triangle window, he called to Demi, "Hey, what are you doing?" His answer was a pivot and stare. The shotgun, aimed toward the roof was slowly lowered and focused on the bed of his truck.

Mr. Nachmann stamped on the accelerator and floored the truck hearing a "Vrroom" followed by an explosion of shots hitting metal. He reached his house in a matter of seconds, and called to his wife who had appeared in the doorway to see who sped up the dirt driveway.

"Call the sheriff. There's someone shooting all the windows out of the farmhouse." Mrs. Nachmann did as she was told, and Marika, Philanthe and the girls surrounded her anxiously to find out what the emergency was.

"Come quickly," she shouted into the phone. "Some man is shooting all the windows out of the Petros farmhouse. Hasbrouck Road. Me? I am Mrs. Nachmann. I lived down the road. Yes, the egg farm."

Philanthe looked at Marika who knew right away who this man was. Demi. They hugged each other and gathered the girls to them. "He doesn't know where we are," Marika consoled her.

"The sheriff will be here soon. You stay right here."

Tugging on Marika's skirt, Helen reminded her mother, "Our suitcase and stuff is at the house. My coloring books from Theo…"

"We'll get the valise and your clothes another time. You have plenty of clothes at home," Marika reassured her youngest child who was shaking and crying.

Trying to be strong for the sake of her children, Marika tried to think, but she could not move her mind from the gold bracelet of daisies, a gift from Petros that stayed in the jeweler's box on the dresser. She dared not wear it. Demi would not understand

Damages

Two people can prolong a marriage long after the marriage should have ended. Marika and Demi shared their house with their children. They both loved Ann and Helen, but they no longer loved each other. Demi continued to spend more and more hours away from home, which was just fine with Marika. When her husband walked out the door of their shared apartment, she breathed deeply and enjoyed the air of freedom. While the girls were at school, she would dress up in her very best and stroll the avenue, window shopping and talking to other shoppers. Sometimes she would walk to the park and sit on the benches for hours watching the squirrels and birds.

She felt relieved to be herself now that Demi no longer cared about her love, only her obedience. She no longer had to enter into the discussions about her infidelity or defend her happiness. She let silence be her reply. "How can I ever convince him that I have no feelings for my uncle other than fondness? He is jealous of my family and hates me wanting to be a part of it."

Demi's defense, when arrested, was that he was defending his family's honor. "Philotimo, Philotimo," Demi shouted at the arresting officer, who had no idea what the Greek word meant. <u>Philotimo</u> is a word that summed up Demi's inbred sense of integrity, public image and what should be right.

Together Philanthe and her daughter kept all the details of the arrest, hearing and probation from the girls. Marika became his *accomplice in the vandalism by pretending all was okay for the sake of the children. All they perceived is that their mother was so much nicer when their father was at work.*

There would be no summer at the farm this year. Demi had forbidden it. "We have a park nearby, and I will take you to Coney Island this year."

Marika was serving his prison sentence, the sentence he avoided by agreeing to pay concessions for damage, in her own apartment. He apologized and offered to pay for all the windows, seventeen of them, along with the door he destroyed with the butt of the shotgun. The court was masculinely forgiving of a man in a rage of jealousy over a flirtatious wife. At home, Demi was her warden, her guard, and her master. In his mind, he did the honorable thing to protect his family. Marika would not be allowed to visit her family.

"They can come here," Demi pronounced. No one did, except Philanthe who tried to time her visits to her daughter and grandchildren while Demi was at work or one of his meetings.

Return from Creedmore

Now that Marika's sister Carrie had a child of her own, she said she would rather not stay with Demi and the girls while Marika was "gone." This time it was Philanthe who had been staying at Marika's apartment for the past few weeks while Marika was staying, for the third time this year, at Creedmore Mental Hospital.

Marika would sign herself into the hospital when she felt one of the "spells" come over her. She would stay a few days, sometimes as much as two weeks. Philanthe wondered what she did there. What sort of treatment could make you well in such a short period of time? In truth, Marika flourished in the attention given her at the hospital. The doctors listened to her; the nurses attended to her needs. She was given the opportunity to think out loud. She always came out looking more rested and happier than when she went in. Like a chameleon on an olive tree, Marika could turn from brown to green depending on her surroundings. When she was around Demi, she was the helpless child he wanted her to be. When she was at the hospital, she was the star of her self-written drama.

Philanthe felt uncomfortable when Demi was around, but then he wasn't around very much. Her son-in-law navigated the apartment as if on a mission. He spoke only to give orders, and he answered questions in one-sentence grunts. Marika had not married young, but she married too quickly for Philanthe's thinking. Long engagements were not necessary, but Marika seemed blinded by this man who had no family here. "You can always tell what kind of *a husband a man will be by how he treats his mother," Philanthe thought. Marika was swept away by the future of riches that this confident engineer promised. "You can't spend promises of riches." Success was always around the corner, just out of reach, and she could tell that Marika was not satisfied with this walk-up apartment on Sterling Street. Philanthe could sense that things were not good between Marika and Demi. "None of my business," Philanthe reminded herself. "I wish she hadn't jumped into this marriage." Some women are more in love with the idea of marriage than they are to the man they will marry.*

Soon Demi would be out the door, and the girls would bustle about getting ready to spend their day with friends in the neighborhood. The girls were pretty self-sufficient; Ann was thirteen and quite responsible about cooking and cleaning, but Helen was only five and needed a mother. Ann was tired of being that surrogate mother. She was old enough to understand, and nosey enough to eavesdrop and hear the whispers about her mom's problems.

Ann never saw these moods as serious because her mom was always happy when it was just the three girls at home. It was only when her father came home that the mood changed, and the air of their home became so tentative, so uncomfortable. It was like slipping out of comfortable shoes into new high heels that pinched and constrained her toes and might create bunions like YiaYia had on her disfigured feet. With Aunt Carrie or Aunt Libby to dote on their nieces, Helen and Ann enjoyed the spotlight when their mother was "away" for some rest. They liked staying with their aunts who had a snack ready for them after school and who helped them with their homework. They especially liked when their grandmother, Philanthe, came to stay with them. YiYia would tell them stories of Greece and what it was like in the days when she first came to America.

Papa worked late, and, when he was home, he was involved at his desk with piles of doodles and designs for inventions he insisted "will make us rich someday." The invention was to dispense forks, knives and spoons in the popular cafeteria-style restaurants. Horn and Hardart's famous automats inspired small luncheonettes to prepare food ahead for the businessmen who ate a hurried meal for little cost. The invention was drawing some interest, but so much effort and money went into the patent that the financial returns were neither immediate, nor impressive.

The quiet between Demi and Marika was intolerable. Conversations were translations or triangles of communication. "Your father wants you to… your mother needs you to…." The parents spoke to and through their children. Ann knew there was something wrong. Helen played the "Ask your father/ ask your mother game." Marika was tired of that game. The words she wanted to say rattled inside her head and were buried in seething self-pity.

It was a Thursday the last time Marika returned from Creedmore Mental Institution, and Philanthe left that morning knowing that Marika's homecoming would be better off without the audience of a mother-in-law. Hoping to avoid her son-in-law, Philanthe left while the girls were at school. She did not want a ringside seat for the battle she knew was coming when Marika came home. Philanthe took the bus home to Carrie's house to help out with the baby Jimmy, who was just seven months old. Tomorrow she will take the bus to New Paltz to visit Petros and enjoy the precious end-of-summer days with warm days and cool nights.

As she walked out of Marika's house, Philanthe shivered, but the chill melted like a raindrop on a cast iron radiator in the warmth and energy of the small apartment in Brooklyn. Carrie's Bill was a good man. A woman could feel safe in his arms. He was eleven years older than Carrie, and sometimes he seemed more like a father than a husband. Carrie didn't need to lean on anyone. She needed someone to walk alongside. Yes, Bill was a good man. Too bad Marika hadn't found a man like Bill instead of Demi.

The Fall of a Marriage

Marika's episodes of paranoia responded to the shock therapy she received at the mental institution. She would endure the painful procedure as a self-inflicted penance for being the bad wife and mother that Demi reminded her she was. A fleeting twinge of agony was the physical atonement for her mental desire to be out of this marriage that fell so short of her expectations. Too bad that there wasn't any medicine that would smooth out those rough spots when she was positive that her husband had someone following her to the grocers, to the dentist, to the school. Just the attention she received and the opportunity to tell the doctors her thoughts and feelings helped to soothe the feeling of impending doom. They understood this "jealousy/control thing" that Demi had over her like a big, black umbrella, blotting out the sun. It was his non-violent way to make her subservient to him. "Great!" she mulled, "Now that I understand how he wields his power over me, what can I do about it?"

Demi borrowed a car to pick Marika up from the Mental Institution. Marika entered the black sedan as if she were returning home from a week at a Catskill resort instead of a release from an institution with a reputation of a warehouse for the scourge of homeless or crazies removed from the streets of society. They rode home in silence. Marika was bubbling over with things she wanted to tell him, but those thoughts crashed when Demi said, "So, are you better? Sometimes, I think you go there for the attention. Or is there a doctor you have your eye on?"

There had been a time she had a crush on her dentist. He talked to her and was so good looking. It was only a crush, a fantasy about a man who treated her as a person with valuable thoughts and ideas. Demi read her buoyant mood and accused her of having an affair. In truth, Marika wasn't looking for romance, just friendship. She and Demi had ceased to be lovers or friends. They were rivals for the girls' love since they had no love of their own.

Breaking the weighty silence, Marika asked Demi about the girls and their first days at school. She should have known better than to touch on the subject that had set off the argument that drove her to commit herself for help for the third time this year. "Did they wear their new outfits?" remembering that Philanthe had given Demi money to take the girls clothes shopping. The girls always had new outfits for that first day back, and Philanthe liked being their benefactor for this special occasion.

"Not this year," he sneered flaunting the fact that Marika wasn't here to take them clothes shopping.

"But my mother gave us money to buy new outfits." Marika had challenged when Demi told her the girls looked perfectly fine in the dresses hanging in the closet from last spring.

"Didn't Annie complain?"

"Of course, she did." Demi mimicked his daughter saying, "It doesn't fit, and I can't wear that. My friends would remember."

"Why couldn't you or YiYia take them shopping?"

"You know I don't have time to take them shopping." He never mentioned spending the "new outfit" money on the Stetson hat in his closet.

Philanthe, who was an accomplished seamstress, had offered to remake dresses for the girls' back-to-school outfits. "I'd rather not. That's too much trouble," Annie balked trying not to hurt her grandmother's feelings.

Demi huffed as he thought about Philanthe taking the girls shopping for clothes. He snarled at Marika saying, "Your mom has no idea of the importance of looking just right for friends to admire. Their own mother should have taken them shopping."

Marika thought of her mother who wore the widow's black cotton YiYia dress like a uniform. Tuesday's dress was just a cleaner, pressed version of Monday's dress. Her mom would never see the importance of being in fashion. "Demi's right," she knew. "I am a bad mother. I should have been here to take them shopping."

She reminded herself that she was a bad wife, hating the invisible leash he held on the imaginary dog collar constricting her voice, preventing her from saying what she wanted to say for fear…for fear, of what she was not sure. She just needed to get away from him. Screaming in her head, she'd hear Demi play that old broken record about how inadequate she was and how no one appreciated his genius and how he was going to be rich when one of his patents was manufactured. In truth, he had some very practical and innovative ideas. What he lacked was the direction to pursue any of them to completion. "Pie in the sky." Philanthe would say about her son-in-law. "He can go to the bank in his mind, but that doesn't pay the bills."

She had committed herself to the mental institution this time. In truth, it was a safe haven from her husband. It was the first week of school, and the girls needed her. The dread she felt made her choose safety over motherly responsibility. She could feel the hatred he harbored for her and was not surprised when he said he wanted a divorce. At first she felt a sense of freedom. A divorce would break those invisible chains she felt that tripped her and choked her when he was around, and sometimes when he wasn't. She wouldn't have to feel that sick to her stomach churning when it was time for him to come home. Yes, a divorce might be just what she needed.

She remembered that night so vividly. It was the week before school had started. The summer had seemed so endless in the city. There were too many hours of pretense. All the fun was orchestrated and planned by Demi for the girls. Marika could well have been mistaken for the governess accompanying her charges on an outing. Marika preferred the routine of work, school, and housework. She, more than the girls, missed the carefree weeks of vacation at the farm.

Demi had come home after ten. Already in bed, Marika heard him slam the door and walk directly to the bedroom. The light switch was punctuation to his decree, "Marika, I need to end this. The girls need a mother, and I need a wife I can trust. I've arranged to see the lawyer." He said this as a pronouncement of a decision made and done. In another country in another time, he would put her shoes outside the door, and that would be final. The marriage was over. He turned off the light leaving her in the dark to decide what to do next. She heard the door slam once more.

The next morning Demi called to tell her that he would arrange for a lawyer to draw up divorce papers. Demi calmly pointed out that the court would surely grant him custody considering her unstable bouts with reality.

"No, you will not get my girls," she screamed into the receiver of the telephone. "If you leave us. You leave all of us. Just get out of my life."

She thought about calling her sisters but decided not to. Instead she called her mother knowing that Philanthe would be able to watch the girls. "Mom, I need you to come and stay with Ann and Helen. I need to go back for treatment. I feel like my life is coming apart." She did not mention the divorce or that Demi demanded custody.

Unglued, she checked herself in at Creedmore to sort things out. That was two weeks ago as summer was ending. As the days closed in on her homecoming, she tried to hide the feeling of dread. She missed her girls, but she knew her mom was there to care from them. If only Demi were gone.

The girls were still at school, so they were spared the strained homecoming. After dropping her bag in their bedroom, Marika walked back to parlor where Demi was staring out the window. He turned toward his wife, shook his head while narrowing his eyes as he stared at her and hissed, "What kind of a mother misses the beginning of a new term of school?" He then walked the short distance to the door and left saying, "Tell the girls I had to work out of town."

The next day, Friday, the girls were at school. Demi came to the apartment to make sure Marika was home and would show up on that night at the lawyer's office. "I'm serious, Marika. I can't live like this. The girls can't have a mother who is not there for them. You just have to sign the papers. The girls and I will go away. You can go live with your mother or some man who would have you."

When Demi had stopped loving Marika, he stopped loving her mother too. Love is a mirror. Demi only saw his own reflection. He no longer saw the woman he had once loved.

"I'll call to remind you of the lawyer's appointment, " Demi said as he left her waiting for Ann and Helen to come home from school. "Tell the girls I had to work late."

A Fatal Friday Night

Modern Greeks no longer worship the ancient gods and goddesses, but the myths of ancient Greece permeate the culture today. Greeks say, "*Siga, Siga,*" which loosely translated means "So, So. A little this, a little that." Every sign points to the middle road. Everything should be done in moderation. There should be no excesses. "Hubris" is excessive pride. If one is "too full of oneself," the gods will surely knock you to your senses.

There is also the undercurrent of fate. Do not challenge your destiny. My mom's favorite saying was, "If you're meant to hang, you won't drown." Unfortunately, her fate was lung cancer, and one of her last attempts at humor with a raspy voice was, "Damn those Lucky Strikes." She would then give us a history lesson about how you could put a quarter in the cigarette machine, and the machine would spit out a pack with three pennies stuck under the cellophane wrapper. She went on to say, "You could even buy "loosies" or "Lucy's" for a penny at the candy store. Now, years after she died, I find myself cursing under my breath, "Damn those Lucky Strikes."

Cursing one's fate was blasphemy. Greeks accepted life as it came. "Hills and valleys," my *YiYia* would say. "Life is a banquet, and you taste it all. Sometimes it's good, and sometimes it is bad, but you go on eating until you cannot."

I cannot understand how Philanthe and my family could go on smiling in the face of such tragedy. I guess it must be an acceptance of life as Yin and Yang, the bad and the good, the dark and the light, death and life.

To understand this senseless murder, you might have to recall the myth of Hercules, called Heracles in Greek. Hercules was a hero, a demi-god. His mother was mortal, and his father was none other than Zeus, king of the gods. Hera was Zeus's very jealous wife, and she had good reason to be. Her husband was always screwing around with some mortal wench down on earth. This "wench du jour" was Alcmena, and the love child of their union was Heracles, reputed to be the strongest man on earth. As his fame grew (hubris), so did Hera's jealousy. She, using her magical powers, drove Heracles insane. He grew raving mad and saw his children and wife as "mad beasts." Ironically, he slew these beasts to protect his family. When he realized what he had done, he sought the oracle at Delphi to see what he could do to atone for his crime. This is where the Hercules of Saturday morning cartoons comes to public knowledge. Hercules had to perform twelve impossible labors to save his own life.

Perhaps the ancient gods drove Demi insane enough to do what he did.

On September 16 of 1944 in Queens, Peter Demetrakoupoulos, Demi, came home from the movies to find his wife Marika sitting outside on the top stoop of their apartment house, slumped over moaning as if she were in great pain. "Are you okay?" he asked afraid she was just having a meltdown as she had before when he had brought up the subject of divorce.

"They're gone."

"Who's gone?"

"Annie. Helen. They're gone."

"Gone where?" Demi asked cautiously as he tried to help her up from that tight knot of confusion and obvious pain.

"Dead. Both dead."

"*What do you mean dead?*" *Demi shot back. Then he paused, grabbed her chin so he could see her eyes. "What did you do?"*

"*Nothing! I did nothing. I shook them. They wouldn't wake up.*"

He ran into the house and could smell that sickening sweet smell the gas company mixed with its gas to detect leaks. He rushed past his wife sitting on the top step and flung open the front door. He ran frantically looking for the girls.

"*Where are they, Marika?*"

He found them lying together in their beds in the bedroom the children shared. He gasped as he saw the lifeless forms that did not react to his screams. He ran to the kitchen to get water. As he ran the tap water into a pot that was nearby, he noticed that the oven door was open. Two burners were also hissing without a flame. He smashed the pot into the window spilling water all over himself and the wall. He kicked the oven door closed and turned off the controls of the hissing burners. His own throat was feeling constricted and sore as he heard himself in a whisper that escaped as a scream, "No. No!"

He threw the water on the girls trying to revive them. They did not breathe as he poked and shook them. He clutched the younger Helen to his chest and then gently placed her beside her sister.

He opened the bedroom windows.

Running back to the kitchen, he grabbed the bottle of vinegar. He would use that as smelling salts. He doused them shouting, "Wake up! Get up!" Even as he punched the mattress by their heads, they only lay lifeless as rag dolls left out in the rain.

His beautiful daughters were dead lying in one bed facing each other with Ann's arm thrown over Helen's shoulder.

Demi could hear the sobs as Marika entered the kitchen. He did not wait for her explanation. He did not care if it was an accident or murder. What did it matter? Marika had let his children die. Without taking his eyes off of her, he reached into a drawer and took out the scissor used to cut up chickens. It came apart in two pieces. He used the one scissor in his right hand to stab her sixteen times. Some wounds were in her chest as he looked into her eyes filled with shock and horror. Some wounds were in her shoulders and back as she tried to get away. He left her to bleed out on the black and white linoleum floor.

Instead of calling the police, he wiped the scissor on a kitchen towel and threw it beside Marika. He called a taxi, and stuffed one half of the scissors in his right pocket. As an after-thought he picked up the scissor half by Marika, wiped it again since it lay in a pooling stain of blood, and put the other half in his suit jacket inside pocket.

He locked the door and waited downstairs for the taxi that would drive him upstate to the farm in New Paltz. Someone would pay for this loss. He needed revenge. Whatever imagined evil he saw in his wife and children was in the blood of the Takis family. He was convinced that Petros was having an affair with his wife. It was a matter of honor. The payment for blood is blood. Someone had taken something from him. He needed to take something in return. Like Hercules, he was raving mad.

On a bridge across the Hudson River, when the taxi slowed down enough, Demi rolled down the window and threw the scissors from his jacket pocket into the water. He found comfort as he caressed the other half that rested, point down, in the right hand pocket of his overcoat.

"I need some air," Demi explained to the driver. "I need to get to my uncle's house. My uncle is dying."

Sympathetically the taxi driver drove Demi through the early morning of Friday night. Demi pretended to sleep rather than converse. It was almost dawn when they reached New Paltz.

Philanthe and Petros, her brother, were in New Paltz this beautiful fall weekend. The farm belonged to Petros, but he was single and shared it with the whole family. It was the retreat from city life. At first it had no electricity, no phone, no water, but it had the most magnificent view and fifty-two acres of open farmland. It had long since ceased to be a farm, but you could imagine the barn filled with cows, pigs, and chickens. The loft held stray vestiges of hay. When Petros moved up during the war, he modernized it and just raised chickens. A small victory kitchen garden near the kitchen had richer soil than the fields of wild grass that grew, uncut, from the house to the barn.

It was close to the road, so cars and trucks could just pull into a dirt driveway that caused visitors to use the kitchen door as the main entrance. The real front of the house faced the curve in the road. No one would park there, so the front walk became overgrown fieldstones, and the porch led to a front door that only seemed to open out to the porch, never in.

You could hear any car approach, and you could count the number of cars that might go down that road on one hand. This car was traveling too fast. It made the right angle turn into the driveway at driving speed causing the brakes to squeal and the car to slant into a car parked close to the kitchen door. Demi handed the driver eleven dollars and got out.

Eyewitness to Murder "Philanthe and brother Petros on porch in New Paltz"

Eyewitness to Murder

Philanthe, who was mid-fifty and matronly, managed to roll herself under the bed as the adrenalin surged in her blood and her heart pounded so loudly that she feared he would hear her hiding there. The bed was a twin bed closest to the window that faced the giant maple tree that brought afternoon shade to the front porch. Just an hour ago she was sitting on that porch in her cotton housedress sharing a cup of real coffee, rare in these days of war, with her younger brother Petros. He had surprised her by picking some Queen Anne's Lace and yellow Yarrow, which turned out to be Golden Rod, and placing them in a Mason Jar on the oilcloth cover on the picnic table.

Now she was squished into a space that was only tall enough to slip a tattered valise under the wire bed frame. "Whose valise was that anyway?" she mused as if it mattered. The handle of the suitcase was digging into her shoulder as she lay on her stomach under the twin bed. The sleeve of the black dress of her other shoulder was stuck on a wayward wire spring. "He should dust more often," she thought *as she stifled a sneeze that was combination of gasps of terror and inhaling a summer's worth of dust and mouse dirt.*

Today they were expecting Gregory and Georgia and their son Nick to come for the day, but not until noon. Gregory was the older brother of Petros and Philanthe. Today was the day that they were to meet with the Sheriff to collect the $300.00 that Philanthe's son-in-law, Demi, was ordered to pay for the damages to the farmhouse. In a rage he had shot out seventeen windows and both doors of Petros' farmhouse. Gregory was coming to be a support in case Demi lost control at the police station in New Paltz as he did in court when the accusation of incest was made as Demi insisted he needed to avenge his wife's honor. He claimed Petros has made advances toward Marika, and Demi had threatened the sheriff and undersheriff when the charges were dismissed with no evidence but his raging jealousy.

Philanthe and Petros expected their relatives for lunch, but at eight a taxi pulled up to the kitchen door. Philanthe, embarrassed in her housecoat rather than her black widow's "YiYia" dress, went upstairs to the largest bedroom to change clothes. Petros walked through the dining room into the farm kitchen and outside to see who was coming so early on a Saturday morning. Philanthe could hear the screech of the screen door and heard the car pull away down the dirt road.

At first there were voices in a conversational tone. "Oh, my God, It's Demi." She realized as she heard the familiar voice of her son-in-law. Petros allowed him into the kitchen. "What is he doing here? He was told never to come here again." She did not quite understand what a restraining order was, but she knew he was not wanted here after he lost his temper and caused such damage while Petros was at work at the defense plant in Poughkeepsie.

A neighbor had tried to intervene when he heard the multiple gunshots at his home down the road. When the neighbor drove up to the farmhouse, Demi had brandished the rifle and shot at the neighbor's car as it approached. The arrest and court appearance just intensified Demi's anger. Demi was convinced that there was something going on between his wife and her Uncle Petros.

Then there was shouting and shoving as the two men tangled and stumbled into the dining room. The dining room table, which over-filled the space of the room and was there to comfortably seat ten or more, cramped the walking space. The two men, close in age, bumped and tumbled over excess chairs, as they squeezed through the doorway to the front porch. Dishes crashed as Petros careened off the glass door of the corner cupboard.

Philanthe froze and listened to them breathlessly curse and push each other. Petros seemed to be trying to explain himself as Demi called him "A home wrecker." Petros managed to get out of Demi's hold on his shirt.

Philanthe ran to the window to see the two men, both in their forties, chasing each other as if they were children playing tag. Petros rounded the old, gnarled tree that hid him from Demi for just a moment. The tree was ancient and large in girth.

Philanthe thought back to May when her daughter Marika, Demi's wife, and their two children played "Ring around a Rosie" at that same tree. Philanthe remembered sitting on the porch watching as the three girls barely circled the tree with their arms outspread. She remembered thinking that they might scrape their bare arms on the rough bark of the tree as they spun around singing with giggling abandon. Now that laughter and singing was replaced with the shouts and grunts of two men engaged in a battle of rage.

Petros spun off and crossed the narrow dirt road to run around the side of the farmhouse. Philanthe glided to the window there. Her brother seemed to look up to the window where he knew she was. When Demi passed under the window, she could see the glint of a silver metal object in his hand.

The two men rounded the house and Petros ran toward the barn. It was a football field away from the kitchen door, and by September the field grasses were knee high except where a path was worn from kitchen door to barn door. Petros made the right angle turns, even though it was longer, while Demi cut into the hay when he saw where Petros was headed. Luckily Demi tripped, and Petros ran ahead.

Philanthe, forgetting her arthritic and aching bunions, ran barefoot to the next bedroom that looked out toward the barn. "Why is he going there?" She wondered. Then she realized that there would be farm implements in the barn. Petros might arm himself. An ax or hoe or even a shovel might make it a fair fight against the knife of Demi.

She stood there transfixed as she watched the two men disappear into the darkness of the open barn door. There were distant noises, all unintelligible but angry sounding. Minutes later, she saw Demi walk slowly, looking back over his shoulder toward the barn.

In horror, she realized that her younger brother had tried to lead this insane man away from her. She crossed to the front bedroom with her shoes in her hands and slid under the bed.

Philanthe was like a helpless turtle wedged under the iron bed. Lying on her stomach, her round middle filled the space between the dusty wooden floor and the spring frame that held the faded ticking of the mattress. She tried inching her way up to the headboard by hunching herself up on her elbows. She could feel a draft on her bare feet so she knew they must have been sticking out the end of the bed. There was no room to curl them out of sight without dragging them forward with her entire being.

The slushing sound she made as she slid toward the cream-colored metal headboard was magnified in her temples as they coursed with blood energized in fear. Although she was barely five foot tall, she felt like she stretched the entire length of the bed. She strained to hear what Demi would do next.

"But he doesn't know I am here," she consoled herself knowing that he wouldn't search the house if he expected that Petros, who was unmarried, was alone. She commanded herself to be quiet. She tried to steady her own breath, but it echoed in her chest in an unnatural rhythm to each pulse of her heart. Her lungs and heart fought each other for space in her heaving bosom.

Sucking in air through flared nostrils, she tried to let her brain control her breathing as she tried to collect her thoughts. She consoled herself with the realization that Demi wouldn't know that she was here. She hadn't told Marika that she was riding up to the farm with her older brother Gregory who was coming up to talk to Petros about the meeting at the sheriff's office. Gregory's son, Nick, was studying to be a lawyer, so the two men wanted to prepare Petros for what would happen on Saturday when Petros and Demi were to settle this damage suit out of court. Petros was such a soft touch, he was likely to drop the charges and not take the $300.00 from Demi who would be hard pressed to come up with that sum of cash. After all, the money would deprive Marika and her children of funds. Gregory wanted to make sure that Demi made restitution to pay for that rampage of insane jealousy. Philanthe just wished it didn't happen. More than that, she said to herself what she dared not say to Marika, "Why did you marry that man? Who shoots out windows with a rifle? Certainly not a sane man." Philanthe shivered with the thought of what might have happened to Petros. "Damn him," she thought. "Demi is nothing but trouble."

She heard the whine of the kitchen screen door as Demi entered the farmhouse.

He was in the kitchen now.

"The coffee cups. He will notice two coffee cups in the old kitchen sink," she gasped, but then remembered that she had taken hers upstairs when she came up to dress. She could picture it on the bare dresser that held an old wind-up alarm clock that was ticking furiously like a metronome clicking in counterpoint to her heartbeat. She strained to hear. The cacophony of the unsynchronized lub/dub of her heartbeat and the external tick tock of the clock blurred the words that floated in pulsating syllables up the stairwell. She couldn't concentrate. Was Petros dead or lying somewhere needing her help?

She turned her head to tune one ear toward the door by the staircase. As she turned, she caught her hair, which was tightly wound up in a cone shaped bun, on the wire frame. She stifled a moan and swallowed an "ouch" as she tugged leaving some wisps of gray strings as she freed her head to listen.

She heard footsteps as he walked into the dining room.

"Dear God, don't let him come up the stairs." She prayed knowing that her son-in-law would want to leave this place as soon as possible before anyone noticed that Petros was gone.

Demi had arranged to be picked up at 10:00 a.m. by the taxi driver that had driven him all the way from Poughkeepsie. He had given the driver $11.00 and promised him $12.00 to pick him up again to take him to the train.

"What time was it now?" she wondered. She tried to retrace the events. Not more than twenty minutes could have passed since Demi showed up.

Demi was dialing. Philanthe could hear the dial as it screeched back to its comma shaped dial stop. "Who was he calling?" She thought as she caught fragments of a conversation that was barked into the receiver.

"Come sooner. I know I said ten. Can't you come now? I don't want to hang around. No, my uncle was not here. Good." He was calling the taxi that had been hired for the round trip to Poughkeepsie.

Philanthe heard him hang up the phone. Moments later she heard the slam and after groan of the screen door as it closed, bounced open and came to rest with a quieter slam. Demi must be outside.

She couldn't see him, but Demi was sitting, legs crossed, on one of the two red metal lawn chairs just outside the kitchen door. He would wait for the taxi. If anyone drove by, he looked as if he were waiting for Petros to walk out through the kitchen door with iced tea and cookies. He lit a cigarette and blew smoke rings, which defiled the crisp country air.

Philanthe allowed herself another deep breath and choked on the stale air that remained under the bed.

She was relieved that he was going. Wanting to run to Petros who was hurt, or worse dead, she was a prisoner fearing both the safety of her prison and her release. What would she find? Thank *goodness, Gregory and Nick weren't expected until noon. The legal proceedings were not until three in the afternoon. She thought of the chicken salad sitting in the refrigerator along with the iced tea and homemade pickles. She had planned on lunch on the porch on this fine fall day. The memory of food caused her stomach to release a foul tasting mixture of digested toast and bile. "What if Gregory comes earlier?"*

Philanthe's mind escaped the horror of the moment by recalling a time, a very long time ago, when she was three and she hid under her bed in the farmhouse in Prosilio. She thought if she stayed there long enough, the strangers would just go away and leave her there. Now, hiding under the bed, she felt three, once again, and frightened.

Ten Children of Nicholas
and Kalliope Tritakis

Demetris married Zaharenia
    No children

Vassilios: (born 1874-1962)
    Kalliope (1903-2002)
    Three boys who died young
    Stellios (1911-2004)
    Panagoiotis (1915-2009)
    Evangelos (1919-1990)

Aristomenes (born 1882) and Pepitsa (born1893):
Twin girls who died during the Spanish Flu Epidemic (1917)
    Kalliope (Poppi) (1914-1931)
    Helen (1916-2008)
    Minerva (Min) (1921-2006)

Philanthe (1886-1970) and George Kontolefa (died 1935)
    Eleftheria "Libby" (1904)
    Marika (1906 –1944)
    Kalliope (Carrie) (1917-2009)
    Peter (1919-2005)

Panagiotis (Peter) (1889-1974) married and divorced a German woman

Gregory (1892-1981) and Georgia:
    Kalliope (Poppi) (1926-died as a teenager)
    Nicholas (1924-1994)

Evdokia married Kalogerakos

Panagiota Tritakis Cofinas
    John
    Kyriakos
    Costas
    Demetris
    Catherine
    Eleni

Another sister

Petros: (1899-1944)   unmarried

1893 Gytheon, Greece

A couple from Gytheon rode up the mountain to visit relatives in Prosilio, which was called Strudza back then. Strudza was the Turkish name for the village, so it has been renamed the Greek word _Prosilio_, which means "toward the sun."

The Tritakis house was one of the first homesteads on the one road that was both ingress and egress to the rest of the farms in the village. Philanthe and her older siblings were playing tag in and out of the dirt road that passes just feet from their front door. Philanthe was three, and she was petite and animated as she chased after her brothers.

Her squeals might have summoned the strangers' attention on the way up the mountain. She was a cute little girl, smaller than the more stocky females of the village. She had blue eyes, and her hair was fair, not dark like the brown-haired Greeks of the area. They were just a few nautical miles from Crete, and the southern Greeks on the nearby island might have been inbred with the Turks. Homogenization is life's progress in warfare. Somehow love wins out, and the human race is strengthened by its own weaknesses as victim and victor mingle throughout history.

Philanthe was fair. She, lover of flowers, was the recessive child of the northern Greek lineage. Her mother, father and nine older siblings were dark and sturdy like olive trees that had anchored themselves to the rocky ledges of the small village centuries ago.

The couple, Voula and Christos, must have discussed this sweet child because they stopped at the farmhouse and spoke to Kalliope. "We have no children, and my husband is old. We have a house not far from the market place. Could we have this little one called Philanthe? Her brothers and sisters can visit. She can go to school and fill our home with her presence. Her life will be better than here."

Kalliope called out the back door to her husband. He recognized this man and called him "uncle." Was he really an uncle? Whose uncle? Did Nicholas have a relative from the village that she did not know about?

"Why do you want this child? You have no farm to work, nor children to tend." Nicholas mused why an older man, obviously older than he or his wife would want to take on the burden and expensive of a small child.

"My wife Voula cries for lack of a child. All her friends have children whose noise livens a home. My wife spends her time with neighbors because the silence of our house threatens her while I am tending the boats. Her day is not full enough."

"But Philanthe will be lonely," Kalliope thought out loud. "Here she has eight older brothers and sisters to play with when they finish their work in the fields."

"But in Gytheon, Philanthe can walk two streets over and go to school. Many girls now go to school. Besides, I can teach her to read and write and sew and do sums because I have been tutored in these," said Voula.

"She can always go home if she wants. She can visit her family or leave if she does not like living with us."

"My wife has friends with children her age. She will not be lonely." Christos was making a concession as he changed his plan. "It's not like she would not be your daughter. She could be our charge. Surely, you would want the best for this pretty little child."

Kalliope was the first to consider the arrangement. What is there about a mother's love that would sacrifice for the child? "And she could visit her siblings, and they could visit there?"

"Of course. She is young. We can call her siblings 'her cousins.' She can still be part of an extended family."

"We will talk," replied Nicholas. "When will you come back up the mountain?"

"We will be back in two weeks to visit our friend. Consider her life and how much better it will be," Christos reminded Nicholas. Without shaking hands, Voula and Christos climbed into the donkey cart and headed down to the sea.

When they reached home, Voula and Christos looked about their modest but comfortable home. A child would fill this space with noise and laughter. She could have her own bedroom, not share a bed with two sisters. There were children her age in the neighborhood, and the school was directly below the house. Since their house was on the third street up from the sea, one could look down over the agora, over the school and into the expanse of sea. The thought consumed them, but they only spoke it aloud once. Voula asked, "Did you mean it? Do you think they would give her to us?"

"Perhaps," Christos responded. "Perhaps they will think of her first." Not another word was said as they headed to bed.

Christos was up before Voula. He let her sleep. The day was too long for her. Not enough to do. Christos rose with the sun and began his daily routine. He dressed quietly and walked the two streets to the main road in town.

Christos owned two fishing boats. Sometimes he would net the small, sweet octopi by himself, but mostly now he let his two helpers take the boats and nets and only go to the docks in the morning to assess the sea and the weather and then in the evening to measure the catch. In between, he would sit first at one taverna and then another. This one he chose that day had the best coffee served with warm goat's milk. Before daylight the taverna's owner's wife would bake honey cookies. He would watch the merchants drying the kalamari on racks along the shore. He would feel pride or suffer jealousy if their catch was inferior or better than his.

Then he would walk up and down the piers and watch the boats on the horizon. He would walk further to watch the ferry from

Crete unload its passengers. Some came here to visit. Some were here to trade their wares at the agora, the open-air market at the end of the block.

Christos passed the agora on his way home at noon. As he wove his way in and through the stands and booths, he picked up some heavy clusters of grapes the color of the pink of baby's cheeks. He thought once again of Philanthe. "I bet she was a cute little baby. Too bad we couldn't just get a baby to raise. But I am old. I would be dead before I could see her married. This child will be there for Voula after I am gone. She will not be a lonely widow. She will be a mother planning her daughter's wedding and hoping for grandchildren." He bought the cluster of grapes. "I bet these came from the farm next door to the Tritakis farm. He waters his vines by hand from the stream. He walked the street that led him home where Voula would be preparing a light lunch of salad with feta and olives.

Voula had risen late and skipped breakfast. She had walked to the agora for some olive oil that was pressed from the olive orchards on the mountain above them. She brought her own jug to fill from the bung of the barrel of the merchant. Like most Greeks, shopping was a daily and social occasion. Some things, like olive oil and the rich wine vinegar, were staples in the kitchen. The maroon color and rich flavor of the grapes complemented the dark oil that she preferred. Some people think that the first light pressing of olives is the best. Voula cared not that her friends taunted her saying she could afford the lightest oil now that she was married to Christos. She was used to the taste of the greener and thicker liquid. Besides, the thicker oil and the acidic vinegar had eye appeal as they streamed and pooled on the salad plate. She would pick fresh oregano from her own herb garden.

At lunch, the older man and younger woman discussed Philanthe as though they were about to acquire a pet. He brought out the responsibility that would fall on Voula as she cared for and instructed their "daughter" in etiquette, in crafts, and in reading. Voula dwelled on the things she would now be able to do with her friends who had children of their own. The house they shared would be a lively place. They would speak to Nicholas next weekend.

Philanthe pretended she hadn't heard the conversation. Her quiet mood went unnoticed in the confusion of so many children. When the couple returned two weeks later, Philanthe hid under the bed she shared with her sisters. Her parents found her and carried her to the donkey cart of the strangers.

"I can't believe that they agreed and just gave her to us," Voula admitted.

"They had her belongings gathered together and seemed to have come to terms with the agreement," Christos said cautiously, withholding the fact that he had sweetened the deal with an amount of money that was unimportant to him but very important to a farmer with ten children, a farmer rich in sky but poor in fertile ground.

Philanthe was told that she would be able to visit with her family and her "cousins" who were, in truth, her siblings. Like a potted plant, Philanthe, the lover of flowers, was transplanted to the town below. The doting of her adoptive parents was like fertilizer to this child who had shared only a fraction of her real parents' time and love. She thrived and basked in the sunshine with the nourishment of good food, education and friendship that Christos and Voula could provide.

Her older brothers would visit her when they came to town. Her parents would check on her when they, occasionally, came to the agora. Philanthe had both family and extended family. Her life improved. She didn't feel deserted. She flourished in this environment for seven years. Then Christos died.

When Aris and Gregory made the trek down the mountain to swim and be with their teenage friends in Gytheon, they stopped by to see Philanthe. She was alone in the house, sitting at the kitchen table. Her blue eyes were ringed with pink, and she looked like she had been crying.

"Where is Voula? Where is Christos?"

"Christos died," Philanthe sobbed. "Voula said it was because he was old, but I watched him grow thinner and weaker in the past few months. He couldn't even walk to the pier without becoming winded."

"So where is Voula? Is she arranging the funeral?"

"No, they buried him at sea three weeks ago. It was his wish to be taken out once more upon the sea and dropped over the side. His fisherman did this for him. I wasn't allowed to go, and my mother could not bring herself to go either."

"Why are you here alone with these bundles?"

"A relative of Christos, his nephew-- I think, will move into this house next week," Philanthe said looking lost and hopeless.

"But where is your mother?"

"She told me to stay here and gather my belongings."

"Why? Where are you going? Won't your nephew let you and Voula stay in this house?"

"Voula is at the church. She is getting married again. She met a rich widower who has two boys. They said I can stay with them and be part of his family. He has a house in the town by the Diros water caves."

"The water caves are over twenty kilometers away. I know," said Aris. *"I went to the caves once by donkey cart."*

The brothers looked at each other, and, without speaking, each knew what the other was thinking. Aris and Gregory both grabbed Philanthe by a hand and scooped up her bundles. Their shorter sister dangled between her taller brothers as they lifted her up and pulled her out of the chair. *"You come home with us."* Uprooted like a weed, held between her older brothers, Philanthe made the long walk up the mountain to her childhood home. She never saw Voula again, and Voula never inquired after her "daughter." Philanthe was nine and brave.

Philanthe Finds Petros

Time, which had sped up as a life was ended in a matter of minutes, now slowed down to a surreal pace. Even though she heard the taxi pull away, Philanthe lay paralyzed in her hiding place. She crawled out from under the bed and walked on the balls of her bare feet to the windows in each bedroom. No car. No sound. Still she waited in the bedroom, marbleized in fear of what she would find when she walked downstairs.

"Shoes," she thought, "I'll need shoes to walk through the hay field," and grabbed them from under the bed where she had left them. She carried them and grabbed her cotton stockings from the dresser. She walked to the bedroom facing the barn. "Nothing," she thought to herself. "No noise. Maybe he's hiding." She consoled herself with the brighter possibilities knowing full well, in her heart, that her younger brother lay dead somewhere out there.

Wearily, Philanthe lowered herself to the bed and very slowly and deliberately put on the cotton stockings and rolled them down around her ankles. Groaning to reach around her distended belly, she reached down leaning to one side to slip into those black shoes that had conformed, over the years, to her bunion shaped feet. She tied each shoe with a bow and walked down the stairs, placing first one foot and then the second on each stair. The banister was her support, for she now felt weak and queasy.

Once downstairs, she cautiously made her way to the kitchen and out the kitchen door. With the energy of a teenager, Philanthe flew to the barn. She called out, "Petros. Petros, where are you?" Only her shaky voice broke the silence of the morning. On the weathered gray barn flooring was a bloodstain where flies had already gathered to suck up life's protein. Her brother had led his murderer inside the barn and to the left of the open barn door.

Philanthe ran out into the sunshine and shielded her eyes that had just become adjusted to the darkened barn. Rounding the barn, she saw her brother's body in the brambles. Tall Joe Pye Weeds, in full bloom of mauve blossoms, formed a cathedral around his head as he lay face turned toward the sky with eyes open and fixed on his destination. Philanthe knew he was dead before she reached him.

She sat beside him, picked up his head and cradled it in her lap as she did when he was young. She cooed and moaned and apologized, "This is my fault. You were drawn into Marika's problems. It is my curse that brought this to you." For the first time today, she allowed herself to think of Marika, her daughter, who was surely in danger. "Demi is crazy. I must warn Marika."

She gently placed Petros' head on the ground, and as she bent to kiss him, she confirmed that there was no breath. When she stood up, which she had to do so from all fours, she saw the splash of crimson on her housecoat. She sucked in air to replenish her lungs and give her the nerve to look at the mortal wounds in his chest. So many times he had been stabbed. She tried to count them. One, two, three, four…she counted the gashes as if she were taking inventory. What did it matter how many times? He was dead.

Instead of going back in the farmhouse, Philanthe ran around the curve and down the road to the egg lady's house. What was her name? When she began to put thoughts together, she would remember that the first house on the right belonged to Nachmann whose husband had heard the gunshots last spring when Demi shot out all the windows and doors of the farmhouse. Later, the police said that was a good move since Demi's fingerprints on the phone were not defiled. She never thought of that. She just needed to escape. She needed help. She needed to call the police. She needed to warn Marika. She ran, but her lungs ran out of oxygen. She doubled up, clutching her belly when she stopped to catch her breath. Her thoughts were all mixed up with another time, another man and another murder in Greece. She had been a widow for a dozen years, but she remembered George, her husband, just as he was when they had met in Prosilio.

Philanthe's Courtship

In the six years that Philanthe had been away, her mother had two more children. Then Kalliope died. Years of childbearing and childrearing took her life early. Nicholas had spawned a dozen children and was left without a wife to cook the meals and work the garden and care for the younger ones. When her brothers brought Philanthe home, it was not just the heroic rescue of their sister; it was the answer to his need. The little ones needed a mother. The boys needed rescue from running both farm and family. Philanthe became the nanny of her own little sister and brother Petros.

The older boys, Aristomenes, Gregory, and Vasilio made their way to America. News of a land of opportunity was abuzz in the harbor town of Gytheon. People there came on the ferry from Crete and brought news of relatives who had gone to America, especially New York, with nothing but an address of a contact and had found jobs and made fortunes.

The three brothers sailed to Crete and then to Piraeus, the port of Athens. They shared a room in Brooklyn, sold food at Coney Island, and saved their money to buy "The Store" on Delancey Street in Manhattan. With profits from the store, they became partners in a restaurant named Gregory's. With each success, they brought over brothers and cousins and founded new restaurants. It was the turn of the century, and everything seemed like an opportunity to become rich and independent.

Their bankroll increased, and they looked for new investments. The poor farmer's children of Greece became the entrepreneurs of New York and Brooklyn.

Philanthe stayed in Greece caring for her younger siblings. Like the most hardy of flowers, she grew where she was planted. One day, when she was sixteen, she was taking the donkey to a far field to graze. She was riding the beast since the field was uphill. All of a sudden, a boy jumped out of the bushes and said, "Shh, don't be afraid!"

"Too late for that!" Philanthe gasped, then screamed.

"Stop that! I need to talk to you," her ambusher whispered in a very loud yet commanding whisper.

It was then that Philanthe recognized George from the farm beyond the church.

"The *proxenitris*, marriage arranger, is going to go to your father tomorrow to ask for your hand in marriage. You are supposed to marry my brother."

"How do you know this?" she asked.

"I overheard my parents and brother talking. That is why I needed to talk to you."

"I don't understand," Philanthe said. "Why are you telling me?"

"I am telling you that you need to tell your father to say 'No.' I want to marry you myself."

With that announcement, the gangly and frightened George disappeared into the bushes and ran away.

"What a crazy boy!" Philanthe thought to herself. Yet she was flattered to be wanted. As she walked home after delivering the donkey, she wondered if this boy knew what he was saying.

Marriage was not something she had even considered. If she married here, her life would just be more of the same. In fact, she hadn't thought beyond today. She felt as if her life was not hers to determine. She was a puppet with others controlling the strings. Her husband would find her. Her own family would be her future. Secretly, she envied her three older brothers who had gone to America.

Sure enough, George was right. The next day the marriage broker came to speak to Nicholas, Philanthe's father. Although the marriage could be arranged without her consent, Philanthe was asked about this match.

"No," she said. "I do not want to marry this man."

Thinking that she was too young at sixteen to marry, Philanthe's father rejected this proposal. Besides, her father needed someone to mother the youngest two children. For another year, Philanthe stayed at the farmhouse with her family.

The next time the *proxenetis* came to the Tritakis farmhouse, it was a proposal from George. She accepted.

Foreshadows

The sun rises and the sun sets in this village where the mountains meet the sun. Daily, weekly, monthly and yearly, today was pretty much like yesterday. Philanthe and George moved into a familiar pattern of caring for each other and the two girls who came along. The oldest was Eleanor who was always called "Libby," and the second was named Marika.

Even this isolated mountain village began to feel the vibrations of an unsettled world. Even Gytheon saw a few cars. Radio brought them news of countries lining up against other countries. America, which once seemed so foreign, now seemed tied to Europe in economics and politics.

George was anxious to leave for America. Aristomenes said he would sponsor George, and George could run the candy factory and store. He, Philanthe and the two girls could live in the apartments above the shop. They were unheated, but the heat from the store, which sold confections and sodas, should waft up the registers to make it comfortable enough. The plan was to go in a year after they had saved up enough money needed to sail to New York.

The compromise was to move down to the town of Gytheon, the home of Philanthe's childhood.

Then it happened. George and Philanthe were just out walking along the piers with the two little girls when a sailor poked his buddy and said pointing to Philanthe, "There she is.

She used to live with Christos and Voula. Her whore of a mother married the first man that came along. Probably been sleeping with him all along. The old man couldn't satisfy that bitch. Neither she nor her new husband wanted the little bastard."

George sucked in his breath, and Philanthe pulled him back as he lunged forward to go after the man who maligned Philanthe and the woman who raised her. He allowed her to command him, turned around and walked his family home.

Later, as Philanthe was putting the girls to bed, George went out to find the man who disrespected his wife and the adopted family who raised her. He found the sailor in a taverna by the ferry to Hania. The man was sloppy drunk and was sitting with a woman drinking Retsina, a wine made from pine pitch, from a plain tumbler.

Without a word, George hit him on the jaw and sent him reeling backward off the wooden chair. George hit him again while the man was still off balance and trying to pull himself up by the table leg.

When the man was upright and leaning on the table, George said, "That was my wife you were talking about, you wretch. You'll think twice about using that mouth to curse another woman." George used a fist to hit him in the mouth. The upward motion also hit the man's nose causing blood to spurt all over him and the men who were trying to pull him away from the drunken sailor.

Bloodied but avenged, George walked home to his family. He knew Philanthe had loved both Christos and Voula. He slept feeling that he had done what any husband would have done if someone insulted his wife.

Before the sun rose, neighbors came to his house the next to tell him that the sailor had died. That punch to the nose had driven a sliver of bone right into the brain.

The trip to America was hurried up to that week. George moved Philanthe and the girls back up the mountain. Once his family was safely back in the village of Prosilio, he sailed to

America. He would work at her brother's confectionary store on Delancey Street in Manhattan, and, when he had saved enough, he would arrange for Philanthe and the girls to join him.

Three years later in 1916, when Philanthe was thirty, she came to America with Libby who was ten and Marika who was eight. Philanthe's older brothers met her and the two girls at Ellis Island to take them to their new home above the store. Once again, Philanthe was transplanted and reunited with her husband, George. Her roots were torn up from the shores of Greece and sown in a neighborhood of apartments above shops in the concrete garden of New York City.

SLAYING OF 4 LAID TO HONOR MOTIVE
New York Times (1857-Current file); Sep 18, 1944; ProQuest Historical
pg. 21

SLAYING OF 4 LAID TO HONOR MOTIVE

Queens Woman Who Murdered 2 Children Had Accused Her Uncle, Slain by Husband

HER DEATH CONSEQUENCE

Machinist Held Without Bail on Homicide Charge Explains Crimes, Police Say

A modern Greek tragedy moved toward its close yesterday with the arraignment in Queens Felony Court of Peter Demetrakoupoulos for the fatal stabbing of his wife, Mary, in their home at 82-10 Rockaway Boulevard, Ozone Park, Queens, in retribution for her killing of their two daughters.

At the Felony Court hearing, which resulted in the holding of the 43-year-old machinist without bail on a short affidavit charging homicide, were two State policemen who returned later to Ulster County, where authorities are preparing a murder case against Demetrakoupoulos for the fatal stabbing of his wife's uncle, Peter Takis.

The companion blades of a pair of scissors brought death to Mrs. Demetrakoupoulos and her uncle Saturday. Demetrakoupoulos told the police he had stabbed his wife to death with one blade, broken the scissors apart and discarded the bloodstained shear, and then gone to New Paltz, where he plunged the bright blade four times into the body of Takis, whom he found working on his farm.

Wife Had Accused Uncle

There had been bad blood between the two men since early this year when Mrs. Demetrakoupoulos, who had been a patient at mental institutions intermittently for several years, told her husband that her uncle had made immoral advances to her on the farm last January. The hatred that smoldered in the machinist's heart had blazed into murderous violence when his wife told him early Saturday she had slain their daughters, Annie, 13, and Helen, 5, because of the "disgrace" visited upon the family by the uncle.

An autopsy at the Queens Morgue yesterday disclosed that the children had died of gas poisoning. This corrected the first impression that they had died by drowning. Assistant Medical Examiner Jacob Werne, who had said Saturday that a superficial examination indicated drowning, explained yesterday that the water-shriveled condition of the children's hands and the wetness of their bodies when found by police on a bed in their home, had been caused by the father's frantic efforts to revive them. He had rubbed them with water and vinegar after finding the bodies.

Was Patient at Creedmoor

It also was disclosed yesterday that the woman had been discharged only last Thursday from Creedmoor Hospital. Hospital authorities said she was released because she was considered able to perform her household duties.

Sixteen stab wounds were found in the woman's body, one in the throat, eight in the chest, six in the back and one in the right side. Any one of several would have been fatal, Dr. Werne said. The three bodies were removed late yesterday to the funeral parlor of George Constantinides, 186 South Oxford Street, Brooklyn.

Assistant District Attorney Albert E. Short said neither half of the murder scissors had been found. Demetrakoupoulos told the police he had thrown one blade into the street before making the trip by taxicab to Ulster County and had thrown the second blade into the Hudson River from the Poughkeepsie Bridge on the return trip.

At the court hearing, Magistrate Peter M. Horn asked the machinist:

"You want to get this over with in a hurry?"

The defendant nodded his head and said, "Yes."

The case is expected to go to the grand jury this week, according to District Attorney Charles P. Sullivan.

The Day of the Funeral

Philanthe did not attend the funeral of her daughter, her two granddaughters, and her brother. She couldn't. The men attended to the necessary ceremony. Sorrow had not yet arrived. Horror and disbelief numbed the brothers, brother-in-laws, and uncles of Marika, Ann, Helen, and Petros.

The caskets were borne by pallbearers who carried one heavy load, just to repeat the sad hoist three more times. Only a few relatives came to hear the priest attempt to convey comfort to the shocked family members. Four coffins, small and large, were placed side by side. Marika's daughters flanked her in their smaller versions of caskets. Only the casket of Petros was opened. His name, Takis, stood separate from the three others labeled Demetrakoupoulos. Two family names had been torn apart by jealousy and united in death. The mourners were the same, mostly male, and all feeling quadrupled grief.

After the final prayers, the Queens district attorney ushered Demi, who was handcuffed, into the George Constantinides Funeral Home. He had accused his wife of murdering the children, and the court allowed him to say his final good-byes to his children.

There was a gasp when he was escorted to the caskets and then whisked away. The police quickly sensed the palpable hatred in the room and turned Peter Demetrakoupoulos, Demi, away from Petros's brothers and nephews who represented the Takis family. In handcuffs and leg irons, Demi was removed from his family and *from the memory of his in-laws. Before sentencing in any court, he was declared dead by Philanthe and her siblings.*

There was nothing left to do for the mourning relatives but to push past the horde of curious people who had come to gawk at the reality of the tabloid headlines that touted this Greek Tragedy. Nothing remained but to accompany the dead to the cemetery then to go home to their families who waited for their men like their ancestors awaited the sailors return from the sea. Home was the safe harbor. The world outside the home was cruel and dangerous. At home the women would have supper and drinks. They would collapse into that safety net of life's necessary routines of eating, sleeping, and beginning the next day with quiet sadness.

Libby, Philanthe's oldest daughter, was at home with her daughter Patty. Children did not need to know such sadness. They would be declared dead, an accident, an unfortunate accident. Patty didn't need to know. Libby's husband, Fotti, was the family's representative, pallbearer and mourner.

Peter, Philanthe's son, had to return from his Army service in Belgium. Usually, a soldier was only informed of a death in the family after the fact, but this was not just an unexpected passing: this was a tragedy, and the government realized that Peter would need to get home to sort out the legal red tape for his Greek born mother and sisters. His long journey did not let him return in time for the funeral. He arrived three days later to have the sad task of signing the death certificates. Carrie's husband Bill had to retell the story. Which story should he tell? Demi said Marika killed the girls. Philanthe thought Demi killed them all. The police didn't really care. They had their criminal. Once Demi confessed to two murders, the case was really done. He would receive the worst possible sentence for one murder. Two times or four times a man's life, what difference did it make? His life was over. He would spend his life in prison or in some insane asylum. Still the family held Demi responsible for all four deaths.

Philanthe had spent the last few days at her daughter Carrie's apartment on St. John's Street in Brooklyn. Carrie's husband Bill, always Vassili to Philanthe, was the crutch to lean on. "Such a good man," she would say to herself and to her daughter.

Bill would guide her through this, and her brothers will deal with the police. She was done with the killings. Here there was life. Jimmy was seven months old. He could sit, smile, laugh and cry. He needed care. As he sat in the wooden high chair in the small kitchen, Philanthe watched as Carrie spooned oatmeal and applesauce into his bird-like mouth. There was no conversation. Both mother and grandmother focused in silence at this squirming child so eager to feed himself that his flailing caused most of the food to decorate his bib and tray.

"Let me," Philanthe said breaking the uncomfortable quiet.

"Are you sure?" Carrie asked knowing that Philanthe's youngest child, Peter—her "diamond", was thirty-two and a soldier. Sadly, she remembered that Philanthe had spoon-fed little Helen just five years before. Burying that thought, she nodded to her mother.

"Of, course, do you think you forget?" she replied taking the baby spoon from her daughter and edging her out of the chair facing the high chair. "You never forget. Never." She dipped the spoon first into the oatmeal, then into the applesauce so Jimmy would taste the sweet before the bland. "And I think I will have a cup of coffee now. Do you have any ground or instant? I can drink it black if you have no sugar or milk." She whispered loving phrases in Greek to her grandson. She would sigh so deeply that her chest heaved until she could dredge up another endearing hope for the life that was unfolding before her.

"When did they say Peter would be home?" Philanthe asked her daughter Carrie.

"He's on his way now. He was stationed a long way from here."

"Does he know what happened?"

"He knows that his sister Marika is dead and that you need him home. It's a special leave, but the military red tape and the

distance make it all difficult. There's no way to talk to him, so he just knows that there was an accident that killed his sister."

"He is going to be so angry," Philanthe said shaking her head and wringing her hands on the apron she was wearing over her black cotton dress.

"Bill will pick him up at Grand Central Station and will tell him the whole awful story on the ride here."

"I am surprised he was able to come home…with the war and all." Philanthe mused.

"I think they made an exception because you may need to be put on the witness stand and need his support for translation… certainly for support."

"I hope they put Demi away forever. I never want to look at him again."

"You might have to. You are the only eyewitness."

"But what about Marika and the girls? He said that Marika killed them. Why would he say that? It's the word of a madman. There's no one left to tell the story. Could Marika kill her own children?" There were so many questions, and Philanthe knew she would not like any of the answers.

"I don't think so, but there were times when Marika was not herself. Marika was crazy, but I can't imagine her killing her girls. She adored them. Maybe it was an accident, leaving the gas stove on."

"Enough…enough about dolofonia (killing)! What's done is done. They are all gone. What does it matter who killed who? It is over."

Philanthe untied her apron and smoothed her widow-of-George black dress. What she could not untie was the knot in her chest that she had tied out of the grief of losing a brother, a daughter, and two lovely grand daughters. There was no revenge in the sentence of her son-in-law to a life imprisonment in a mental institution. Revenge was too strong an emotion for a woman who had mustered such courage to live, and now wondered what she had to live for.

Just then Jimmy wailed to be picked up as Carrie was talking to her sister Libby on the phone. Philanthe walked slowly to the high chair, hoisted the pudgy boy out of the tray and held him tight with both arms. She cried softly as he screamed loudly until they both sang the same song of sighs and sweet whispers. She walked to the window that overlooked the busy street below. With the curtain parted, a ray of sun shone on Jimmy as she settled into the rocker and sang a lullaby in Greek. The music calmed both listener and singer. The lyrics were as fresh as they were when Philanthe sang to her own babies: Libby, Carrie, Peter, and, sadly, Marika.

Philanthe with Libby, Marika, Carrie and Peter

Philanthe as a Mother

Working at the candy factory, George made a decent living. Libby, who was a teenager, would work after school to bring in some extra money. Her job was to dip the chocolates and box them. Each chocolate candy had its signature swirl that marked the chocolate covered cherries from the coconut crèmes. The young couple, George and Philanthe, lived rent-free in the apartment atop the factory and retail store with Libby and Marika and then Carrie and then Peter, the son born in 1919 who would carry on the Kontolefa name.

There was no heat in the tenement apartment except what lofted through the ceiling of the candy store below. Sometimes they would leave the cook stove burners on to throw enough heat in the compact kitchen so the diapers of the babies would not freeze in the pail. They saved all that they could hoping that someday they would have their own apartment, perhaps in Brooklyn or Queens. They wanted a place with a backyard where the children could play with other children in the neighborhood and walk to school. They appreciated the generosity of Aris, Philanthe's brother, but George *always felt beholden. "I want to pay rent so I feel the place is mine," he explained to Philanthe.*

Once a week, after the children were tucked in for the night, Philanthe's brothers and George would have a poker game and enjoy some illegal liquor at Philanthe's dining room table before going home for the night. The stakes were higher than George could afford, but he would play a few hands and then help his wife serve peanuts and small cakes to their guests. It was the players' tradition to leave the last pot's ante for Philanthe.

She saved these coins until she had $20.00, enough for a pedal sewing machine, a Singer she saw in the Sears and Roebuck catalogue. George ordered if for her, and she proudly paid for it with her earnings. At the time it was an extravagance, although she said it would save money if she could make more of the children's clothing. She never knew at the time that the sewing machine would enable her to provide for her children when her husband died of stomach cancer when Peter was just sixteen.

Philanthe sewed and mended and paid the rent in an apartment in Brooklyn with a yard in a neighborhood where the four children could walk to school.

Philanthe and Carrie and Peter

Philanthe's Son

When a woman is a widow, she relies on her children if she is fortunate enough to have them. Philanthe had four children. Now she had three. With Marika gone, Philanthe was passed back and forth, like a shared family heirloom, from Carrie to Libby and then back again. She became the baby sitter, the companion, and the extended family to her son and daughters, mostly her daughters.

Philanthe's son was on the front lines of a war. Ordinarily, the Army would deliver the bad news of a family death after the fact with solemn protocol causing grief to be put second to a soldier's duty. In this case, the Army made an exception knowing that Peter was the only son and would be needed. In the meantime, Carrie's husband stood in as the manly crutch for a woman whose life had just been turned into unimaginable turmoil. It would be Carrie's Bill who would break the news to Peter about his sister, uncle and nieces.

A woman can share the emotion of grief with another woman, but not with a man, at least not in the same way. A woman *has the ability to look into the soul of another woman and reflect that sadness with the touch of a hand, a hug, or eye contact. Men deflect real feelings from a testosterone shield that doesn't allow the emotion in or out; instead they radiate bravado that speaks insincerity. A man suppresses the real emotion and buries it under a false mask of strength. Philanthe's brothers were consumed with revenge and hatred for Demi, and that anger trumped sadness. Philanthe knew that none of this would bring Marika and either egkoni, granddaughter, back from the dead.*

During the days leading up to the funerals, Philanthe sought the silent sympathy of her daughters' company. She left the trappings of grief to her brothers and nephews who expressed that sadness in anger and quiet hatred. Instead of tears, their reactions were visible in the jaw line betrayed by clenched and grinding teeth.

Once the funerals were over, she relinquished her strength to her son Peter. Peter was her youngest child. He was named after Petros, her youngest brother who was murdered just five days ago. Philanthe called Peter "her little diamond" which she pronounced "dee a mund." Peter was her family jewel. He was the Kontolefa namesake. He was the affectionate reminder of a man who once loved her before he shriveled and disappeared into the invalid who preferred to sit in the dark corner of their apartment and shunned visitors. Only a teenager when his father George died of stomach cancer, Peter's only memory of his father was that of an old man sitting in a wooden wheelchair with a plaid, wool blanket on his lap.

"Could it have been just a week?" Philanthe mused thinking back to all the horror that those days could hold. "Just last Thursday I was riding upstate to New Paltz, a trip that left crowded houses and city noise for the quiet of rolling hills and mountains." Listening to the katydids, she had slept peacefully in her brother's farmhouse as Marika, Annie and Helen were murdered on Friday night. As she slept, her son-in-law unleashed his rage in his plan to stab Petros on Saturday morning. Saturday and Sunday was a blur of police and refuge of family. Monday and Tuesday were funeral arrangements, a

strange funeral with four bodies and only men there to represent the family and mourn with grief overshadowed with loathing.

Insulated from the image of death, the women and children busied themselves with the banal, autonomic actions of life. There were meals to fix for the men would who return hungry from the ordeal. Beds needed making, and laundry didn't stop just because four lives had ended. Diapers needed folding, and Philanthe's grandson Jimmy needed bottles boiled. Patty, Libby's daughter, needed her dresses ironed, and the phone kept ringing. There was so much living to do in the midst of an over-abundance of death.

Philanthe both appreciated and rejected the attention of her family, but what she longed to do was to be alone to throw herself onto the bed and howl and rage and expel the evil that had invaded her being. "I will not give in to selfish crying," she reminded herself as she forced herself to accept the ministrations of well-meaning friends and relatives.

Now it was Monday, a day Philanthe dreaded because she needed to give statements, once again, to the police. She had managed to face the past days in the sanctuary of her daughters. Today she needed her son who had been allowed to travel home from Belgium. Traveling all the way home from overseas, Peter missed the funeral but had the burdensome task of dealing with the medical examiners, police and press. Although Philanthe spoke English, the shock of losing four family members would not allow her brain to separate Greek from English and fact from feeling. Peter translated as she recounted the events of the murder at the farm in New Paltz for the Queens District Attorney as she had for the Ulster County District Attorney.

The hardest part was answering questions that insinuated that her daughter was "crazy" and that Marika had killed her own children.

"No, never," Philanthe told the skeptical detective. "Marika loved her girls."

"But her husband, your son-in-law, stated that he arrived home to find his wife sobbing hysterically on the front steps." The

pudgy officer leaned forward on his elbows and flushed knowing he was adding insult to injury.

The woman sitting before him looked vacant up to now. Her blue eyes were rheumy and red, but they met his with a determined focus. She spoke with her molars clenched and hissed, "He killed them."

"We have only his statement. He admits killing Marika but not the children."

"They were dead. Gassed. Marika would not do that."

"Perhaps it was an accident?" her son interrupted.

The detective conceded that it was possible since the coroner had determined that the cause of death was illuminating gas, propane from a light or stove. "At this point, it will be up to the courts to decide if Mr. Demetrakoupoulos killed two or four people."

"What does it matter? They are all gone." Philanthe sighed as she put her head in her lap and hugged herself until Peter rose and crossed over to her chair and lifted her like a swaddled child. He held her up until he could feel her straighten and stand firm on her own feet.

"Detective, my mother has told you all she can. It is over. They are all gone. Only Demi is left, and his life is over too." He led Philanthe to the closed door, and as he opened it, he glanced back and said, "I am taking my mother home. She has had enough. The victims are buried, and you have your killer. Do with him what you will. He has destroyed himself and he has destroyed my family." The door slammed as final statement.

They walked along the sidewalk, and Peter held his mother's hand as they left the shadows of the precinct and headed for the bus stop to go to his mother's apartment. It was the first time she would go home. She had not wanted to be alone with her thoughts. They sat for a minute on the curbside bench that faced the park and watched the children play. The bus came and went, and passengers got on and off. Philanthe watched them, unable to summon the effort to get up from the bench to join all those who moved with the determination of a direction. The world seemed to be operating at a speed she could not match with the life force sucked out of her. They would wait for the next bus. Perhaps then they would stand up to be ready to board.

A few tears fell silently down Peter's cheek. Philanthe stared into the sun without even blinking. Her eyes were too dry, and all her tears were gone. Her reservoir of tears was empty.

"How many days did they give you?" she asked of Peter. She knew it was unusual to let a soldier come home from the front lines. This was different. Four of Peter's relatives were devoured by his brother-in-law's insane jealousy.

"Just a week. I have three days left."

"Let's stop at the butcher. I have coupons. I bet you haven't had lamb chops."

"No, I haven't. A soldier's stomach doesn't see the likes of lamb chops."

" Then we shall have four. One will be for me, and three for you, my son. Perhaps we can find a lemon. I have a small jar of olive oil, the good kind…light and clear," Philanthe said with conviction of a mother who provides for her children. "When this war ends, we will have roast lamb and lemon and real butter."

Burial

Philanthe, like all of us, had lost people she loved. She thought back to her adoptive parents. She remembered her own mother who gave her to another woman. She remembered leaving her father and brothers and sister when she fled to America. When George died, she had four children to feed and clothe. Now she had three, but she had two grandchildren, and she would have four more. One grandson would be named George, as is the custom. The son's son is named after the grandfather. Philanthe's first grandson would die young, at twelve, and rest in a grave that reads, "Thy will be done." George's namesake, the son of Pete and Eva, died with the mind of an infant, shielded from the regrets life can deal.

The fates sit ready to snip short the lives we love. We can only mourn and go on.

Limbs had been brutally hacked from her family tree. Such a brutal pruning by the fates could kill that tree. The shock might cause its leaves to wither, its trunk to starve and roots to weaken. The next storm might take it down to rot and return to the earth. A mortally bruised tree stands a better chance if it can seal off that scar and nourish itself with sun and water. Philanthe never again spoke of Marika, although she visited the graves of her daughter and grand daughters. The secret visits were hers alone. She needed no audience and chose not to tell Peter, Libby and Carrie.

No one mentioned the murder or its victims. If the family spoke of them, they did so away from Philanthe. Like bitter pills, the murders were swallowed and excreted. Names were not spoken unless in whispers. Newspapers were trashed, and photographs were hidden away. The men emptied the apartment of all its evidence of the man, woman and two children who no longer lived there. The women tried to fill the void with the present. The past was not to be spoken of if it included Marika's family.

Philanthe buried them in the depths of her memory and she went on for another twenty-six years before she joined them in the ground. Philanthe had seen sadness in the shadows, but she always could face another sunrise. She believed in life and knew that the sun would rise and the shadows would fall behind us. Her family tree, like all living things, can only survive if it seeks the sun.

Philanthe's Flowers

Some plants become hardier as they are nibbled down by deer or put down deeper roots as frost threatens to kill them. Philanthe's roots ran deep, wide and strong. As she rests in the ground, the second and third and even fourth generation in America flourishes because she made that brave journey with two little kids to follow her husband who fled from Greece. She grew wherever she was planted. She seeded a garden of teachers, engineers, investment brokers, and computer whizzes. Her grandson Jim just became a College President. In a family of Americans, her scion of Greek ancestry lives on because her story lives on.

Prosilio

When we Greek-Americans visit Greece, we feel that connection with the land, home of my grandparents, great aunts and uncles. The family farm still is atop the mountain in Prosilio, fifteen kilometers from Gytheon, now a tourist destination. This poem was written when my family, nine of us, visited Gytheon, the home of our grandmother and the place Philanthe lived with her adoptive parents.

Nine on a Beach: Gytheon (1984)

Following vanished footprints
On an ancient beach
Bleached by centuries of searing sun;
A homecoming
A reunion of strangers
Already introduced in memories
And recognized in familiar faces.

Nine on a foreign beach,
A family together for the last time;
A final product
At one with the
Seeds of our beginnings,
Meeting like the turquoise sea and sky
Meet at the shore again and again.

Epilogue

2009

First mom, then Aunt Helen, then Aunt Chris, and finally Aunt Carrie grew old, sick and died. As we cousins gathered at funerals with our own children and grandchildren, we tried to condense our half centuries of courting, marrying, birthing, raising children, traveling and managing careers. We had led fifty years in separate lives tied only by blood and memories of a summer long ago. We tried not to sound like our own verbal obituaries as we recounted our life's choices. Spouse's names and children's names were superfluous. We produced snapshots of families raised apart from each other. We were relatives who gathered at weddings and funerals. We had shared joys and sighs in holiday cards and sporadic phone conversations. If we did not resemble our own parents so much, we could have been hugging balding, graying strangers over paunches and sagging breasts. How could a lifetime with our mothers end so abruptly?

As we moved from polite talk to reminiscing, we returned to the summers we spent at the farm in New Paltz. Launched from the bond of these strong aunts, we were now the adults our aunts hoped we would become—adults who learned to persevere in the shadow of adversity and set admirable goals.

Armed with research skills and curiosity, we shared what we knew about Philanthe's escape from the rage of her son-in-law.

Articles in newspapers answered the questions our young minds forgot to ask.

As I wrote *Prosilio*, I had planned on puzzling out the circumstances of the murders. Did Marika have a crush on her uncle, or did she just crave the attention she couldn't get from a husband who confused love with possession? Could Marika have killed her own children rather than give them up to her husband? What criminal sentence was meted out to this man responsible for ending the lives of four members of my family?

I almost made the mistake of writing the trite television drama that plays out a lurid murder with lawyers and juries. Writing this tragedy in the life of Philanthe, I came to realize that our strength comes, not from revenge, but from using that grief and rage to redouble our resolve to live life to the fullest. I no longer care about the details of a crime and the punishment of a murder.

Marika, Ann, Helen and Petros were characters in a Greek tragedy played out on a stage of another time. That curtain closed to allow other characters to play out their own scenes. It is the drama of Philanthe, and the lives of the next generation of matriarchs, that scripted the summer vacation that taught us our life lesson—Always walk toward the sun, and the shadows will fall behind you.

Acknowledgements

To Aunt Eva Kontolefa who retold the stories of her mother-in-law.

To my book club: Jo Chin, Betsy Deak, MaryAnn Bruck, Gayle Kavanagh, Patty Goodemote, and Kim DiGiovanni who read and improved my rough draft.

To my good friends and neighbors: Bob Tischler, Joe Kosarek and Pat Tosi, who found my typos and added all those missing commas

To my siblings and cousins who shared those summers on the farm that launched us from the shelter of childhood to the independence of adulthood: Kenny and Kathy Olsen, Jimmy and Michael Jacobs, Barbara, Kenny and Gary Gundersen, and Jane and Elaine Vecchione

To the matriarchs: Min, Helen, Chris, and Carrie

To my great aunt Philanthe

Author Biography:

Carol LaMonda is a retired English teacher who taught at Onteora Central Middle and High School. She writes a bi-weekly column entitled "A Jar of Olives" with news and commentary about her hometown, the Town of Olive, which is in the Catskill Mountains in upstate New York. She lives there with her husband Bruce. Her two sons' families live nearby with their children.

"This memoir/biography is the catharsis that marks the passing of a generation of Greek Americans who provided me and my relatives with delightful summer vacations in a farmhouse in New Paltz, New York. The deaths of our parents passed the torch of responsibility to finally search out the family secret of the five murders in the Takis family, one of which took place in that farmhouse where we vacationed as carefree children. In searching for the details of this Greek tragedy, we learned more about Philanthe, a great aunt born in Prosilio, Greece, who witnessed the murder of her youngest brother and lost her daughter and two granddaughters to a jealous son-in-law. What we discovered was that it is possible to survive tragedy if one leaves the shadows and walks toward the sun."